C000164408

Parable Sermons for Children

PARABLE SERMONS FOR CHILDREN.

Parable Sermons for Children.

BY

H. J. WILMOT-BUXTON, M.A.,

VICAR OF S. GILES-IN-THE-WOOD, NORTH DEVON, AUTHOR OF "MISSION SERMONS
FOR A YEAR," "THE LORD'S SONG," "THE LIFE WORTH LIVING,"
"SUNDAY SERMONETTES FOR A YEAR," ETC.

Fifth Edition.

London:

SKEFFINGTON & SON, 163, PICCADILLY, W.

—

1893.

To

SIR JAMES R. FERGUSSON, BART.,

OF

SPITALHAUGH, PEEBLESSHIRE, AND

HEVER COURT, KENT,

THESE SERMONS ARE DEDICATED.

Contents.

Parable Sermons for Children.

SERMON I.

THE THREE PICTURES.

S. MATT. XXV. 15.

"Unto one he gave five talents, to another two, and to another one."

You know, my children, that a parable has been called an earthly story with a Heavenly meaning. Now I am going to tell you an earthly story, and you must try to tell me the Heavenly meaning. The story is about a very famous Artist, who has painted the most wonderful pictures. These pictures are very many, and very different. They are great and small, some dark, others bright ; some make you sing with pleasure when you look at

A

them, others make you cry with terror. One picture shows you the great wide sea, sparkling in the sun, and the shadows of the tall cliffs lying on it. That is a very lovely picture. Then another shows you an earthquake, where the houses and churches in a town have all fallen, and the men and women and little children are buried alive, and the black, threatening sky hangs over all. That is a very terrible picture. One picture is that of a little rosy child playing in a meadow : and another is that of a poor, white-faced lad, lying on his dying bed, his thin hand clasped in his mother's. Sometimes this great Artist has painted very simple pictures, such as a bunch of snowdrops, or a butterfly with gay-coloured wings; but whatsoever He has done, the picture is always *well* done.

Now this great Artist had three sons, and when they were quite little children their Father taught them how to paint. He showed them some of His own pictures, and they learnt to make drawings for themselves. One day the Artist said to His sons, " I am going away on a long journey, I cannot tell you when I shall return, but you must be very industrious, and work hard whilst I am away." Then He led them into His studio, or painting room, which was full of canvas, and easels, and paint-

brushes, and pictures, and models. To each son
the Father gave a piece of canvas to paint on. The
eldest son had the largest piece of canvas, the
second had a smaller piece, and the youngest had
the smallest canvas of all. ·Then said the Artist to
His sons, " You must each try to paint me a good
picture, the best you can, by the day when I come
back to you. You cannot paint equally well, but
you must do the best you can. All your pieces of
canvas are not of the same size, but each is large
enough for the picture which you can paint." Just
before He left them, their Father told them that
there were many pictures which they might copy,
or they might look at the view from the window,
and paint that; but He advised them to make one
particular picture their model. Then He drew
aside a curtain, and showed them the portrait of a
very beautiful Child. The Child was carrying a
white lily in His Hand, and there was a strange, dark
shadow cast before Him. So the Artist went away
on His long journey, and the three sons were left
to their work. The eldest stood before his big
canvas, and thought, "What sort of picture shall I
paint?" At first he determined to draw a grand
battle scene, full of soldiers in gay uniforms, and
plunging horses, and waving flags. Presently, when

he had mixed the colours, and taken the paint
brush, he thought that he would paint a picture of
a king on his throne, with all his lords and great
men standing round him, and he proposed to draw
his own portrait amongst the courtiers of the king.
Then He looked towards the picture of the Beautiful Child, and the Child's eyes seemed to follow
him sadly and reproachfully.   So the young painter
put away all thought of the battle scene and the
court, and set himself to copy the likeness of the
Beautiful Child.   It was very hard work at first.
The Child's face was so pure and lovely, that the
painter felt that he could never imitate it exactly.
Sometimes he grew angry and impatient at failure,
and then he would make ugly blots and stains with
his paint brush on the picture.   Then he was very
sorry, and would kneel down beside his work, and
cry bitterly; and he found, to his surprise, that
wherever his tears fell the ugly blots and stains
disappeared, and he was able to go on with his
painting.   At last the picture was finished, but the
young painter was not satisfied with it.   He felt
that it was not half good enough—but he *had done
his best.*

Now, you remember, children, that the second
son had a smaller picture to paint.   For some time

he did no work, asking himself the question, "What sort of picture shall I make?" He thought to himself that he could not paint anything grand on so small a canvas, so he looked out of the window for a subject. He saw that a fair was being held in the town, music played, flags waved, and people laughed, and danced, and sang. He said, "I will paint the fair." But after a little while the music ceased, and the people went away, and the lights were put out, and the streets were dark, and sad, and deserted. So the boy grew weary of his picture, and determined to paint another. Then he looked at the face of the Beautiful Child, and the gentle eyes seemed to follow him reproachfully. So he set to work to copy the Child's likeness. But he had wasted much time on other subjects, and he made many mistakes in his work, so that he often cried, "I shall never finish my picture in time."

What was the youngest son doing all this time? He looked at his small piece of canvas, and thought —"What is the use of trying to paint on such a little thing as this! No one could make a good picture on it." So he put the canvas away in a drawer, and did not try to do anything with it, but spent all his time in sloth and idleness. One day the great Artist came back quite suddenly. His first words to His sons were, "What work have you done for Me? Show Me your pictures." Then He looked at his eldest son's work, and smiled approvingly, and said, "Well done, thou hast been good and faithful." The second son came with his picture, which was smaller, and on him his Father smiled approvingly, and said, "Well done, thou hast been faithful in a small thing." Last of all came the youngest son, blushing with shame, and carrying his empty canvas in his hand, and his paints and brushes all unused—"I could do nothing with such a little thing," said he, "and so I hid it away out of sight." Then his Father was very sad, and very angry, and He led His two elder sons with Him into a new and beautiful house, where there were more lovely pictures than they had ever yet seen, but the youngest son was shut out.

Now tell me, my children, the Heavenly meaning of this earthly story. The great Artist is God, who has made the Heaven and the earth, and the sea. And the three sons, who are they? We ourselves, and all people in the world. And the pictures which we have to paint are our lives. The painting room is our place in the world, where we

are put to work. And the portrait of the Holy
Child which we have to copy, is the example of the
Lord Jesus Christ. I told you that in the picture
of the Holy Child there was a long dark shadow.
You know what that means ? It is the shadow of
the Cross. That will come into our picture too.
Now remember that every day you live you are
painting a picture—your life ; some of you may be
painting the picture of an ambitious life, full of
battle scenes, and kings, and courtiers ; some of
you may be painting a picture of pleasure and
amusement, like the son who began to make a
picture of the fair. But if you want to make a
really *good* picture, if you want to lead a really good
life, you must try to copy one likeness, that of the
Holy Child Jesus.

SERMON II.

THE BUILDERS.

Psalm cxxvii. 1.

"Unless the Lord build the house, they labour in vain that build it."

I SPOKE to you lately, children, about the great Artist and His pictures. To-day I want to tell you a parable about some builders. There was a famous Architect, who had built great cities, and little villages, marble palaces, and simple thatched cottages. Some of His buildings were very grand, others very simple, but all were alike well built. These houses were let to different people to live in, and some took care of them, and kept them in repair, and others did not. The great Architect had two servants or apprentices in His workshop, and He taught them how to build, and always gave them these three pieces of advice—First, *Always build on a good foundation*. Next, *Always choose good materials*. Thirdly, *Build slowly*. After a time, the great Architect sent His servants into a new country, and told them each to build a good house that would stand. Well, the two servants emigrated to the new country, where they found many other people all building, some well, others badly. One servant remembered his master's advice,—*Build on a good foundation*. So he got workmen together, and searched about for a likely spot to build on. When he found it, he cleared away all the soil and rubbish, until he came to the solid rock, and there he built his house. Remembering his master's advice,—*Always choose good materials*,—he hewed out seven pillars of stone to support the roof, and to each pillar he gave a name. You must try to remember their names. The first pillar was called *Faith*, the second *Obedience*, the third *Love*, the fourth *Truth*, the fifth *Gentleness*, the sixth *Prayer*, and the seventh *Work*. And, again remembering the master's teaching, the servant built *slowly*. On the top of the roof, high over all, he fixed a great stone Cross, so that whenever the sun was shining, the house was under the shadow of the Cross. At last the house was finished.

Now what was the other builder doing? He went to work in a very different way. He laughed at his companion for taking so much pains, and went down to the river-side, where the sand lay smooth and yellow. He determined to built there, and forgot all about His master's advice, and the good foundation. And he forgot also the advice about building slowly, so he hurried on the work, that he might finish his house, and enjoy himself. Neither did he choose good materials for his building, but used any wood or stone which came in his way. Instead of the seven pillars of the house, this builder had but one, and that was called *Selfishness*. The house was finished at last. But there was no Cross to cast its shadow over the building.

The winter came, and the wind roared, and the storms raged, and the floods rose, and beat upon the two houses. The gentle river of summer became a foaming torrent, which dashed against the walls of the buildings. But the waves beat in vain against one house, and in vain the wind shrieked at the windows, and the lightnings flashed, the house stood firm. Why, my children? Because it was founded upon a rock, and was well-built of good materials.

Now let us look at the other house. It seemed strong enough, and safe enough in fair weather, but when the storm came, the sandy foundation began to sink and tremble. The one weak pillar, called *Selfishness*, began to totter and give way, and presently the whole building fell to pieces like a house of cards, and the flood swept away the ruins, and the poor foolish builder with them.

Now we must think of the Heavenly meaning. You know, of course, that God is the great Architect, who has built up all the cities and villages, and the mountains and islands. We are all His servants, and He sends us into this world, a new country, to build. What are we to build ? Good lives, lives which will stand, and last for ever. Remember the lessons of the Architect. First, we must build on a good foundation, and our foundation must be Jesus Christ, the Rock of Ages. There is a text in one of S. Paul's Epistles about this, " Other foundation can no man lay than that is laid, which is Jesus Christ." (1 Cor. iii. 11.)

Next, we must choose good materials to build up our lives with. What are they, do you think ? Good companions, good books, good work, innocent amusement.

And, thirdly, remember to build *slowly*. Good lives are built up by degrees. Great generals, and statesmen, and lawyers, and clergymen, became great slowly by learning, so do good Christians. Then we must remember the seven pillars of our house. Can you tell me their names? The first pillar must be *Faith* in God, making us trust all to Him. And then comes *Obedience*, for if we believe in God we shall try to obey Him. Then there must be *Love*, love to God, and to each other, no good life can be built up without the pillar of Love. Next comes *Truth*. Every noble life is built upon Truth and Honesty. And we must not leave out *Gentleness*, which makes our building so sweet and beautiful; nor *Prayer*, without which we *cannot* make a good building; nor *Work*, that we may be useful ourselves, and be able to help others. These are the seven pillars that keep up a good Christian life. And above all this life, my children, there must be the Cross of Jesus Christ. Our life cannot be good, cannot be what God loves, unless we deny ourselves, and give up our own way; that is living under the shadow of the Cross.

We have looked at the house built on the rock,

the holy life founded on Jesus ; now look at the
house which fell, the life which was lost. The
foundation of sand is this world's pleasure and sin,
the pillar is selfishness, not love, or faith, or
obedience ; a building like that cannot stand
against the storms. Those storms are the temptations, and sorrows, and losses of this life, which
come to all of us. The flood beat against *both*
houses, remember, so troubles and temptations
come to good and bad alike, but only the lives
founded on Jesus can stand against them. Now, I
want you to ask yourselves a very serious question,
What am I building?

SERMON III.

THE THREE GIFTS.

S. MATTHEW II. 11.

"They presented unto Him gifts; gold, and frankincense, and myrrh."

It was the holy season of Epiphany, when the Christ-Child was first shown to the Gentiles. Among the many who went to Church, was a little boy, one who loved no place so well as God's House, with its "dim, religious light," and its fair white columns, and its solemn music. He was a very quiet little boy, and thoughtful beyond his years. His friends said he was a dreamer, and if so, he had very beautiful dreams sometimes. Often he would go into Church alone, when there was no service, and kneel down and think, and perhaps pray. It seemed to him that, when the light streamed through the painted windows, and fell upon his Prayer-Book, he could see Heaven opened, and catch a glimpse of that wondrous City which he had read about in the Revelation of S. John. It seemed, too, that sometimes the pictured saints and angels in the window used to smile upon him, as though they were pleased to see a little boy in Church. But there was one painted window at which the little boy was never tired of looking. It represented the wise men offering their gifts to the Child Christ. Whenever he looked at this picture there was always one thought in his mind—Oh! that I might see Jesus, and that I might give Him an offering! It was the same when the organ pealed through the Church, and the voices of choir and people sang of the Guiding Star, and the gladness with which men of old followed it to find Jesus. The child was always saying to himself—If I could only see Jesus, and take Him a gift! One day, when he had heard the wondrous story of Epiphany over again, the little boy remained in Church, lost in thought. And there seemed to come a dream or vision to Him. He fancied that the organ was being played very soft and low, as though an angel's

fingers were touching the keys, and as the child
gazed on his favourite window, gradually the figures
in it seemed to live, and move. He saw a very
brilliant star, like a comet, shining down from the
sky, and making all the scene bright. The scene
was a rude stable, and the oxen and other animals
were standing there. And they seemed to the
child's eyes to be real living cattle, and to be bowing
their heads reverently before a little Baby, wrapped
up in coarse, poor clothing. At first the little boy
could not see the face of the Babe, but He observed
that She who held Him in her arms was exceeding
beautiful. But presently, as the wondrous light
streamed on the scene, the little boy could see the
features of the Babe, and he thought that they
smiled lovingly upon him. After awhile, the child
saw three strangers kneeling before the Mother and
her Babe, and he knew that they must be the wise
men, the three kings who had come from the East
to worship Jesus. As he watched the wonderful
scene, the child saw the wise men open their stores
of treasure, and the first, kneeling very humbly,
presented his offering of gold to the Holy Babe.
The watching child could see the light flash upon
the precious gift as it was presented. Then the
second stranger drew near, and held in his hand a

kind of silver dish, from which rose a sweet-smelling smoke, and for a moment veiled the scene from the eyes of the child, and he knew that this was the gift of frankincense. Then the third of the strangers approached the manger, and offered something wrapped in a fine linen cloth, and the child noticed that the faces of the Holy Babe and His Mother were sad, so the little boy remembered that this was the gift of myrrh in token of the burial of Jesus. By and by the scene faded away, and the child saw only the painted window as before. But now the longing to see Jesus came upon him stronger than ever, and as he kneeled in Church, he prayed most earnestly—"O Jesus, let me see Thee, and give Thee an offering." Then it seemed to the little boy that someone whispered in his ear, or perhaps he only remembered what he had heard before, but the words came back to him now, "Inasmuch as ye have done it unto the least of these My brethren, ye have done it unto Me." When the child went home, his mother gave him a ripe, rosy apple, and the boy, for he was but a child, and thought as a child, was delighted with the fruit. Just as he was going to eat it, he remembered a poor, sick lad, who lived in a back street in the town. This lad had been a teacher in the Sunday

B

School, and had won the love of all the children by his gentle schooling; specially he loved the little boy of whom I am telling you, and used to call him his little flower. Now the young teacher had been ill for a long time, and there was then no hope that he would ever be well again in this world. .Presently the little boy was standing by the sick lad's bed, and giving him the apple of which he thought so much. It was not much perhaps, but it was all he had, and it brought comfort to the parched lips of the dying teacher.

When next the child went to Church, and heard the glad lessons of Epiphany, he seemed to see once more the vision in the painted window. Once more the wise men brought their offerings, and to his surprise the child saw among the gifts which lay at the feet of Jesus an apple of pure gold. And there came back to him the old words, which the dying teacher had spoke to him, " Inasmuch as ye have done it unto the least of these My brethren, ye have done it unto Me." And so the little boy learnt how he could offer gold to Jesus by doing good to His people. But still he wondered how he could offer frankincense and myrrh, as the wise men had done. That night when he was asleep, the child dreamed a very beautiful dream. He thought an angel came to him, bearing a silver censer in his hand. And as he swung the censer to and fro there went up a cloud of sweet incense. And the angel smiled upon the child, and said, "these are the prayers of all holy children who pray to Jesus, and your prayers of to-day are among them." Then the little boy was very glad, for he knew that he had offered *two* gifts to Jesus—gold and frankincense. But what of the bitter myrrh?

After awhile the young teacher died, and was laid in the Churchyard. The children of his Sunday Class, of which the little boy was one, agreed among themselves, there were seven, that they should deck the grave with flowers each day in turn. And so for a year, the grave of the gentle teacher was tended by loving hands. One morning in summer, very early, when the grave-digger went to his work, he was surprised to find a little child lying asleep upon the grassy mound where the teacher lay buried. The old sexton asked him how he came there, and the little boy answered that on the night before, it was his turn to deck the grave with flowers, and that he could not find any beautiful enough, and so, said the child, "I would not disappoint teacher, and I thought that, as he used to call me his 'little flower,' I would just put myself on his grave, to show how I loved him."

Within awhile another grave was made beside that of the teacher, and on the tiny head stone they carved these words—"Little Flower; he gave himself to show his love."

SERMON IV.

THE TRAVELLERS.

HEBREWS XIII. 14.

" Here we have no continuing city, but we seek one to come."

I AM going to tell you a story which was first told
by the Old Greeks, about a certain King and his
companions, and I want to see if you can find some
lessons and warnings in it. This King travelled
over many lands and seas, and met with many
dangers and wonderful adventures. They had left
their homes to fight in a long and terrible war, in a
foreign land. When the war was over, they longed
to go home again, but many difficulties and dangers
stood between them and their native shores. I will

tell you about some of them.   First, when they had
begun their homeward journey, they met with some
fierce and strong enemies with whom they fought.
Having conquered them and driven them back, the
companions of the King sat down to feast on the
spoils which they had taken. The King, their leader,
who was very wise, begged them to get to their ship
and sail homeward at once, whilst they were safe,
but they would not listen to his advice.   Presently,
whilst they were all feasting, forgetting their danger,
their enemies, who had recovered their strength,
rushed upon them and drove them back, wounding
some of them very severely.   Now the travellers
were glad enough to escape to their ships, and to
carry away their wounded friends to sea.   Well,
they steered their ships towards home, but they met
with tempests and contrary winds, and were driven
about hither and thither, till at last one day they
came in sight of land. They went on shore, and
found the country very beautiful.   The sun was
always shining, the air was hot and sleepy, it was
" a land in which it seemed always afternoon," no
one appeared to do any work, the people lived only
to eat and drink and sleep.   Presently the King and
his companions found out the reason of this.   The
people of this strange land lived on the *lotus-fruit*,

which made them lazy and careless, and forgetful of
everything but their own comfort. The wise leader of
the travellers saw the danger before him. The fruit
was very tempting, the life appeared very pleasant,
if his companions should eat of the lotus they would
forget home, and friends, and duty ; already some of
them were looking longingly on the fatal fruit.

> " Most weary seemed the sea, weary the oar,
> Weary the wandering fields of barren foam ;
> Then some one said—' we will return no more :'
> And all at once they sang—' Our island—home
> Is far beyond the wave, we will no longer roam.' "

Some of the travellers tasted the lotus-fruit, and
at once became as sleepy and idle as the people of
the country. Then their leader determined to act.
He had them seized, and tied with thongs, and
carried by force on board their vessels, then every
sail was set, and they passed away from the
dangerous shores of the lotus-eaters. The travellers
had other troubles in store for them. They came
one day to a wild and rocky shore, very different
from the sweet, flowery land of the lotus. The
people of this country were fierce giants called
Cyclops, who were also cannibals. The King and
his friends soon found themselves prisoners in the
cave of one of them, who killed and devoured a

prisoner every day. Well, at last, when many of
their friends had perished, the travellers managed to
blind the giant, and escape from the cave to the sea.
Joyfully the remainder of the little band got on
board their ships, and as the blind giant came
furiously to the shore, the King mocked at him from
the deck of his vessel. Now in this the King was not
wise. For the giant having cast some great stones
at him without being able to hurt him, uttered some
terrible curses. These curses did a great deal of
mischief, and were the cause of a great many
misfortunes to the travellers, as you shall hear
another day.

Now, my children, I want to see what lessons this
story has for us. I think the old Greeks meant
much of the story to be a parable, at all events, it
shall be one to us. We will think of the king and
his fellow-travellers as being ourselves, all mankind.
We are sent from our home, Heaven, to a long warfare in a foreign land, that is, this world. And we
must conquer all our enemies, and pass through
many trials and dangers, and cross a stormy sea of
temptation before we can reach home. All went
well with the travellers as long as they remembered
their home and their friends. So it is with us,
my children. We are citizens of Heaven, " here

we have no continuing city," we are all "strangers
and pilgrims," and all goes well with us whilst we
think of our home in Heaven, and of our friends
there, God, and the saints and angels. The first
mistake which the travellers made is just the mistake
which we often make. When they had conquered
some enemies, they sat down to feast, instead of
going homewards. Our enemies are our *sins*. If
we struggle hard, and conquer some sin, we must not
sit down at ease, and say, "I am safe." The sin
will attack us again stronger than ever, and when we
think we are standing safely, we shall fall. We
must keep out of the way of temptation. Having
fought with our sin and got the better of it, we must
try to get away from it as far as possible. When
the travellers put to sea on their homeward journey,
they met with storms and tempests. You and I,
my children, have to pass the waves of this troublesome world before we can find our home; and the
troubles, and sorrows, and misfortunes of life are
the storms which will meet us.

After a while the travellers came to the shores
of the lotus-eaters. I wonder if any of us have
been there too? I think that country means the
land of *idleness* and *sloth*, and the fruit of it is *forgetfulness*. Those who eat of it forget their duty, and

their home, and their God. Ah! children, have
none of you tasted that dangerous fruit? When I
see a child idle in school, careless and inattentive in
church, lazy in his work, always thinking of eating
and drinking, and playing, neglecting his prayers
and his Bible, then I know that child has eaten the
fatal fruit, he is forgetting his home and his friends.
What must you do if you *have* tasted the fruit? You
must get away from the dangerous land of idleness
as fast as you can. Put out to sea—the sea of work
and duty—and never mind the stormy weather.

Then again, the travellers fell amongst giants.
Our *bad habits* are our giants, and they keep us
prisoner, and eat us up by degrees. The boy who
uses bad language is living as a prisoner in a dirty
cave with a foul giant. The *idle* child is sleeping
away his life in a cave with his giant. The *deceitful*
child is in a dark place with his giant. The *dishonest
child* hides away his ill-gotten goods in the cave of
his giant. And, sooner or later, the giant, the bad
habit, destroys us. Boys and girls, some of you are
kept prisoner by a giant. Make up your mind, get
out of his cave, there is Some One who is stronger
than the giant. Jesus will help you to escape. But
what is the door out of the giant's cave? *Repentance.*
What is the key to open with? *Prayer.* Use that

golden key now, and it will open for you a door of escape. And when you have got away from the giant, don't mock at it. "Fools make a mock at sin." If you look back and laugh at a bad habit, or an old sin, you will find it will follow after you, and overtake you again. And now may God bless you, and help you to understand these words.

SERMON V.

THE TRAVELLERS. (II.)

HEBREWS XIII. 14.

"Here we have no continuing city, but we seek one to come."

I TOLD you lately, my children, about the king and his fellow-travellers, and some of their adventures in the land of the lotus-eaters, and among those terrible giants the Cyclops. And you will remember what lessons we learnt : that *we* are all travellers on our way home, seeking that Heavenly City which is above; and that we must avoid the dangerous shore of sloth and forgetfulness, and the strong giants, which are Evil Habits.

Now let me tell you some more about the

travellers. When they had escaped from the giants, they sailed away over the lonely, homeless sea, seeking their native land. At length they came to the Country of the Winds, where the king of the winds made them welcome.

Now *we* know, as Christians, that God is the God of all nature, God of the sea, and of the land : of the wind, and of the tempest. We know that " fire and hail, snow and vapours, wind and storm are fulfilling His word." We know that "He hath made summer and winter, and that by Him were all things made, and without Him was not anything made that was made." But the old Greeks, who were heathens, did not know this. They thought that there was one god of the winds, and another of the seas, and another of fire, and so on. When a storm arose they said that the god of the winds had sent forth his servants. When the sea raged, they thought the god of the sea was angry. You must remember this in order to understand me. I suppose that the king of the winds was really only a clever man who invented sails for ships, and so the Greeks made a god of him. Well, this king of the winds was very friendly to the travellers, and when they left him to continue their journey he gave them a leather bag, tied with a silver cord, and containing all the stormy and adverse winds as prisoners. Only the sweet west wind was left out, that it might carry the travellers home. And so they took ship once again, and for nine days all went well with them. Gaily their ships sailed over the sea before the sweet west wind, and the king steered, trusting no other hand on the helm. At last they came within sight of home, they saw the rocky shore, and the green meadows, and waving trees, and the smoke going up from their own houses. Then it was, when they were almost safe in harbour, that the king, tired out with steering, fell asleep. And his companions were tempted by curiosity to examine the bag which held the winds. They thought the silver cord must certainly tie up a treasure, and so in an evil moment they opened the bag. Out rushed the angry winds, and blew their ship far away from home, out of sight of their native land. When the king awoke, instead of seeing his house and friends close to him, he found that they were once more out on the desolate sea, and the winds raging around them.

Now let us look at the Heavenly meaning of this Perhaps we are going on very well for a time, trying to lead good lives, and so getting nearer to God and our Home, when some curiosity tempts us to do something which God has forbidden. Then if we yield to the temptation we are driven, by *a storm of our own making*, far from Home and God, into the dark stormy sea of sin and shame.

You know that Adam and Eve were close to God in their home in Paradise; they had all that they needed; they might eat of all fruits in the garden, except of one tree. That was forbidden. Curiosity tempted them to eat the forbidden fruit, and in consequence they were banished from home, and not only they, but all mankind, were shut out of Paradise. Then "remember Lot's wife." She had come safely out of Sodom, and curiosity tempted her to do what was forbidden, to look back upon the city of sin and pleasure. She looked back, and she perished. Then think of the Prodigal Son. He was safe at home, happy, prosperous, loved by his father. Curiosity tempted him to see more of the world. He wanted to open the bag of the world's pleasures and sins, as the travellers longed to open the bag of the winds. There are many big boys and girls like him. They think it manly to go away from home before they can govern themselves. The boy says, "I want to be my own master." He thinks it a fine thing to get into the bad company of those who drink, and swear, and tell bad stories. He wants to find out all sorts of things which are not good for him to know. Like the foolish travellers he unties the bag, and out rush all the bad passions, and temptations, and evil communications, and carry him away. He finds out what drunkenness means, and what impurity means, and very likely he discovers what dishonesty and disgrace mean. And where is he driven to? To the husks, and the swine, and the foul rags of sin, and the filthy food of a wicked world. And if the prodigal does not come home again penitent to his Father, he is lost utterly.

Oh! boys and girls, don't be curious to find out evil in the world. God will teach you everything which you need to know. Never be curious to look into bad books, or to talk about bad things, or to go to bad places. Remember what curiosity did for the travellers, and try to keep innocency, "for that shall bring you peace at the last."

SERMON VI.

THE TRAVELLERS. (III.)

HEBREWS XIII. 14.

" Here we have no continuing city, but we seek one to come."

Do you remember, my children, how the travellers were punished for their idle curiosity and disobedience? When they opened the bag which held the strong winds they were driven by them away from home. And very soon they fell among giants and cannibals, quite as fierce as their former enemies, the Cyclops. These giants destroyed all the travellers and their ships, except the vessel and crew of the king himself. So the lonely ship sailed away from that terrible shore, and the king and his companions

C

were very cast down and sad, and began to think
that they should never see home again. By and by
they came near land, but they were afraid to venture
on shore lest they should find new enemies.   It
was necessary, however, to get fresh water, so the
king agreed to stay on board his ship, whilst his
officer landed with the crew. They found themselves in a very beautiful country, and soon came in
sight of a palace.   There were pleasant gardens all
round it, bright with flowers, and shaded by fruit
trees.   Instead of seeing dogs or horses near the
palace, the travellers found lions, and tigers, and
bears, and other savage beasts, but they were as
tame and gentle as our cats at home.   This
wonderful place belonged to a famous witch, or
sorceress, and she soon came and invited the
travellers to feast with her.   The officer refused to
enter the palace, but the hungry sailors eagerly
accepted the invitation.   They ate greedily of the
food set before them, but their gluttony was quickly
punished, for the dishes were drugged with magic
herbs, and no sooner had the sailors feasted on
them, than they were turned into a herd of swine.
When the officer saw the fate of his men, he
hastened to tell the king of this new misfortune.
When he had heard the news, the king went on

shore to search for his companions, and as he came near to the palace of the witch a stranger met him, beautiful as an angel, and told him of the dangers of that enchanted spot. Then he gave the king a plant with a white flower, which would protect him against all the arts of the sorceress. After awhile, when the king had entered the palace, and tasted the magic feast, the witch tried to transform him into a beast, but the white flower made him safe, and the witch was conquered. She even consented, at the king's request, to restore his companions to their proper shape.

And now, children, the king and his companions acted very foolishly. Instead of hurrying away from that dangerous place, they stayed for a long time in the palace of the sorceress, but the white flower, which the king carried, kept him safe. At last the travellers remembered their home, and their duty, and set sail once more, but there were many dangers yet before them. They sailed near some shores where they saw some beautiful women sitting upon the sands, singing, and beckoning to them. The song was so wonderful that all who heard it were drawn to the place at once. But those who sang were cruel creatures, called Sirens, who tempted travellers to destruction, and the shore was all

whitened with the bones of those who had listened
to the song, and perished. The king had been
warned of this danger, and he caused his companions to stop their ears with wax, so that they
could not hear the fatal song. He ordered his
crew to bind him to the mast, and on no account to
let him loose. However, he had not stopped his
ears, and when he heard the Siren's song, he wanted
to go on shore, and begged the sailors to loose
him, but fortunately they could not hear him, and
so that danger was passed. By and by the travellers
entered a narrow strait of sea, where there was a
monster on each side, one hidden under a great
rock, the other in a deep whirlpool. And here the
danger was, lest in avoiding one monster, they should
be caught by the other. But after awhile they
passed on, and came to a shore where some cattle
were feeding. Now these cattle were sacred to the
Sun-God, and the king had been specially warned
not to injure them. The travellers were forced by
the stormy weather to remain for some time on land,
and one day, while the king slept, his companions
killed and ate some of the oxen. Then very
terrible things happened. The skins of the slain
animals moved as if alive, and crawled after their
slayers; the meat, whilst roasting on the spits,

seemed to groan and cry, and when the travellers put once more to sea fearful storms arose. The ship was struck by a thunderbolt, and all the crew was lost except the king. He was shipwrecked, and after passing through many more perils, which I cannot tell you about now, he came safe home at last.

And now, my children, let us see what all this teaches us. After their idle curiosity and disobedience the travellers fell among destroying giants. That means just this, that *sin brings its own punishment.* "Our pleasant vices are made the whips to scourge us"; when we sin and suffer for it, we whip ourselves. These giants in the parable are the effects of sin. The drunkard is destroyed by the giant of bad health. The glutton is pursued by the giant of sickness and headache.

And next we learn the lesson of the Enchanted Island. That beautiful, wicked witch is *Sinful Pleasure, or Lust;* one of those things which in your Baptism you promise to renounce, to declare war against. When the travellers had tasted of the witch's food they were turned into beasts. Do you think that so very wonderful? I have often seen the same thing. I have seen a boy—once a bright-faced, honest, simple lad—getting into bad company,

going with companions to the tavern, learning to
become a drunkard.   At first it all seemed to him
as delightful as the witch's magic cup, but look at
the boy presently.   Instead of the bright-eyed,
honest-faced lad, I see a heavy, down-looking
fellow, with flushed, swollen face, and dim, watery
eyes, which are ashamed to look at you straight-
forwardly.   Then I know that the boy has been
turned into a beast.   Or, I see a young girl who
was once modest and pure, regular at Church and
Sunday School.   Now a change has come over
her.   She is scarcely ever at Church or School now.
She has no smiling welcome for the Clergyman;
she tries to avoid him.   Instead of her Hymn Book
she carries a penny book of foolish and immodest
songs.   Instead of her Bible and Prayer Book she
has a false, and often wicked story in her hands.
Instead of spending her evenings at home, she is
running about at night, wearing more ribbons than
she can pay for   And what is the cause of all this?
She has tasted the poisoned cup of sinful pleasure,
and her nature is changed.   Look at the boy who
was once in the choir, singing God's praises; now
he sings filthy and foolish songs; he was a good
boy once, he is changed into a beast now.   O
boys and girls, be warned, don't taste of any pleasure

which is sinful, it is simply poison.   Do you know
how the king escaped from the power of the witch
and her sorcery?   Because he had the white flower,
which is *Temperance.*   You remember what we
are told in the Catechism, that we must keep our
bodies in temperance, soberness and chastity.

Next, remember the shore of the Sirens, who
lured people to destruction with their song.   We
often sail past those shores.   The Sirens are our
Temptations.   Each temptation has its own special
song.   The world has one song, and the flesh
another, and the devil another, and they are sung
to many different tunes.   *Idleness* sings a song to
you, my children, about the pleasure of taking
things easily, and never doing hard work.   *Dishonesty*
sings its song in a soft, low key, and says, "It's
only a trifle, no one will know, take it."   What
must we do, children?   *We must stop our ears.*   Do
not stay to listen, or the temptation may be too
strong for you, and you will fall.   If you are
tempted to look at a bad thing, turn away your
eyes; if you are tempted to listen to a bad thing,
stop your ears.

Now think of the two monsters in the narrow strait.
I told you that in avoiding one, travellers were often
caught by the other.   Well, we all have to take care

lest whilst we keep clear of one sin, we fall into another. One child avoids the sin of Sabbath-breaking, and goes to Church regularly, then he thinks—how much better I am than my neighbour's boy ; what a good boy I am. He has avoided the rock of Sabbath-breaking, but he has gone right into the whirlpool of Pride. You remember the Pharisee in the parable : he fasted, and gave alms, and kept the law, and yet he fell into the whirlpool when he condemned the poor Publican. Try to keep in the *middle course*, children, and look out for the dangers on each side; if you avoid one kind of sin, be on your guard against another.

And now, last of all, when the travellers disobeyed and killed the cattle of the Sun-God, as the Greeks called him, you remember what terrible things happened. We learn there that the sins of the wicked can't be killed, they dog their steps and cry out after them. If you have done wrong, and have not confessed your sin and repented, some horrible thing seems to be crawling after you, some terrible voice seems to be crying out after you. That is the memory of your sin. And now my parable is ended. I have tried to teach you that we are all travellers on a journey through this life, and that we are going home to Paradise, through many dangers,

and difficulties, and temptations. On this journey
we must fight, and watch, and pray, and above all
we must have Jesus as our Guide. He will give us
strength to triumph over the temptations of the
world, and the flesh, and the devil, and will enable us
with pure hearts and minds to follow Him, the
only God.

SERMON VII.

THREE WISHES.

S. Luke XXII. 42.
" Not My will, but Thine, be done.'

Now, my children, I daresay you often wish for things which you have not got. I think we are all of us very fond of wishing. A boy says, " I wish I were a man, and my own master, I would have no more lessons." A girl says, " I wish I had plenty of money, I would ride in a carriage with a pair of horses, and have a new dress every day." Another says, " I wish I could go up to London, and see all the sights, the grand ships, and the fine houses and Churches." I have even heard a very little

child say, "I wish I could fly." Now it is very
natural to wish, but it is often very foolish, because
we wish for what is not good for us. Suppose that
an angel were come into this Church now, and were
to ask each person present what he wished for. I
wonder what sort of answers would be given. I
think one person would wish for plenty of money,
and another for good health, and another would say,
"I wish to have my own way always," and another
would wish for abundance of nice food. But do
you think these are very good wishes? Would the
angel be very pleased with them? No, the answer
which the angel would like to hear would be, "I
wish to be a good servant of Jesus Christ." No
doubt you children have all wished sometimes to
have plenty of money. If you have gone to the
bank, and seen the clerks shovelling the sovereigns
about as carelessly as if they were worth nothing,
no doubt you have wished that you might have a
few shovels full. And when you have read in the
fairy tales about people having sacks full of gold,
some of you have wished that you might have such
sacks of treasure. Well, I am going to tell you a
story of a man who wished to have a great deal of
money, and you will see that such a wish is not
always wise or good.

The story is told by the old Greeks, of whom I
have already spoken.   They tell us how there was a
certain king, who had a palace to live in, and
gardens and fields to cultivate, but who was discon-
tented because some of his neighbours were richer
than he.   The king was always wishing for wealth.
He thought that if he could have boundless riches
he should be perfectly happy.   But he made a great
mistake, as you will see.   Well, he went on wishing
for more money, till one night a vision or dream
came to him.   He saw a stranger, who seemed not
to belong to earth, and who told the king that he
should have his wish, whatever it might be.   Now
I daresay, children, you wish that this could happen
to you.   You think how pleasant it would be to
have anything you might wish for.   Well, I don't
know, it depends whether our wish is a wise one.
You will hear what the king's wish was, and what
came of it.

He thought to himself that the opportunity had
come to him to get wealth, and to become the
richest man in the world.   Then he would never
trouble himself again about his kingdom, or the
affairs of state, for he should be perfectly rich, and
therefore perfectly happy.   So the king told the
stranger of his dream what his wish was: it was

that everything which he touched might be turned into gold. When the morning came, the king was very anxious to see if the vision was true or false. He hurried into the garden, where the roses were blooming, and filling the air with sweetness, and plucked one. No sooner had he touched it, than it became a mass of golden leaves without scent. Then the king was delighted, for he had got his wish. He broke off a bough from a tree, and it became in his hand a solid stick of gold. He touched the ears of corn, already looking golden in the sunshine, and they became heavy metal. He gathered the rosy apples, and they became apples of gold. Then the king thought to himself—" Now I am perfectly happy. There is nothing which money cannot do, and I can turn everything into money." The king began to feel hungry, and went into the room where his morning meal was prepared. But when he took a piece of bread in his hand, it became a lump of gold. He lifted a cup of water to his lips, and the water became solid gold. Then the king began to doubt whether his wish was so very good after all. He looked through the window, and saw his servants enjoying their food, whilst their master was like to be starved. Presently the king's little daughter came in, carrying a bunch of roses for her father. As soon as he took them in his hands they became hard, scentless flowers of gold, and the child began to cry at the change in her favourite roses. The father took his child in his arms to comfort her, and she suddenly began to grow cold and hard, and instead of a living daughter, he clasped a golden image. And now the king saw how fatal his wish was.

When night came, weary and famished, the king lay down on his soft bed, and in an instant it became a piece of hard, slippery gold. All night the poor king lay awake on his hard couch, and he would gladly have changed places with the poorest of his labourers who was sleeping soundly. So the king found out his mistake, and saw how foolish and wicked he had been, and he begged hard that the terrible power of turning things into gold might be taken away. His request was granted, and I think we can fancy how glad he must have been to be able to touch his food, and find that it was not gold, and to put real water to his lips, and to sleep on his soft bed, and to see his daughter restored to him. That king had learned that to be rich need not mean to be happy. He had learnt, what we ought to learn, that the secret of happiness is in doing our duty, and leading a good life, and being contented.

My children, learn to be contented with such
things as God has given you. Then you will be able
to turn all things into gold, only in a better way than
the king did. The contented child will find his
plain food as sweet as a grand dinner served on gold
plate. The contented child will think his simple
clothes as good as though made of cloth of gold.
The child who loves Jesus has always riches, since
" in the house of the righteous is much treasure."

There was a very famous Roman once, who had
gained many victories for the state. He might have
lived in a grand house, and had riches and honour,
but he chose to dwell in a simple cottage near Rome,
and cultivate a little garden. One day messengers
were sent from Rome to take him a present of gold.
They found this great conqueror cooking his simple
supper of vegetables. When they offered him the
present of money, he refused it, saying, that a man
who was contented with so simple a supper had no
need of gold. Learn, then, my children, to be
contented, and everything which you touch will be
better than thousands of gold or silver.

And now let us think of some one else who wished,
and who had his wish granted. He, too, was a king.
One night, when he was lying on his bed, God
appeared to him in a dream, and asked him to

choose whatever he might wish for. You remember
who that was? King Solomon. And you all remember that he chose wisdom, that he might govern
God's people rightly. That is a good wish for us,
that we may be wise to learn God's will, and to do
it, to see God's way, and to walk in it. And now
think of yet One Other. We look on Him kneeling
in a garden, in great agony and sorrow. Drops fall
from His brow like drops of blood. You know of
Whom we are thinking,—the Lord Jesus Christ.
Now He had a right to wish, and to have His wish
granted if ever any one had. Yet hear what He says,
"Not as I will, but as Thou wilt." Now which do
you think is the best example for us to follow? That
of the foolish king who wished that everything he
touched might become gold? Or that of King
Solomon who wished for wisdom; or that of the King
of kings, Jesus Christ, who wished to do the Will of
His Father? I think you will all feel that the best
wish for us is this—" I wish to have no wishes left,
Thy Will, O Lord, be done."

SERMON VIII.

THE STRONG MAN. (I.)

REVELATION XXI. 7.

"He that overcometh shall inherit all things."

THERE lived once among the Greeks a very famous hero, who was the strongest man in the world. It had been foretold that after going through many dangers, enduring many toils, and fighting many battles, he should be taken to Heaven, and dwell among the gods. The name of this hero was Hercules. He was quite a little child when the first danger overtook him. He was lying on his little bed, when two great serpents came into the room. I think you would have been very frightened

D

if you had seen these two terrible monsters, with their gleaming eyes, and long forked tongues, crawling up to your bed. But the child Hercules was not afraid. He seized one snake in each hand, and, so strong was he already, that he crushed them to death.

When he had grown into a young man, Hercules was called upon to make a very important choice. One day he saw two women, one fair and modest, dressed neatly and simply, the other very showy and gay in her appearance, covered with ornaments and jewels. She who wore the showy dress spoke first, and told Hercules that he must choose between her and her companion. If, said she, you make me your choice, you will have a life of ease and pleasure, you will have no work to do, no troubles or cares to vex you, you need do nothing but eat, drink, and sleep, and others will work for you. You will have only to think of yourself, and need never trouble about other people. Well, Hercules thought this sounded very tempting and pleasant; he should have his own way, there would be no one to interfere with him, there would be no hard work, no rough fighting, no wounds, nothing but enjoyment. So he turned to the woman, and asked her name. She answered that by her friends she was called *Pleasure*, others called her *Sin*. Then said Hercules, "Tell me this one thing more. Pleasure cannot last for ever. I shall grow old and weak one day. I shall no longer be able to taste what I eat or what I drink. I shall be too deaf to hear the sound of singing, too feeble to join in the dance. What can you give me then?" The woman confessed that she could give him nothing then. Now she could provide pleasure, but nothing hereafter. Then Hercules turned him to the other, who was called *Virtue*, or *Duty*. She told him that if he chose her as his guide and companion, he must expect to work hard, for there would be difficulties to overcome, and battles to be fought, and victories to be gained. He would have to think of others, to help the weak and suffering, to endure hardness, and to pass through many fiery trials. "And what hereafter?" asked he. And Virtue told him that when his work was over, and his duty done, he should be taken from the earth to rest, from labour to peace, and that rest was only for those who did their duty. Then Hercules thought within himself—Which shall I choose? Pleasure is very tempting; it is very sweet to have one's own way, and to lead a life of ease and comfort. But then what a price to pay for it! To have nothing hereafter; no home of rest

when I am old and worn out. If I choose Virtue
or Duty I must live a life of hardness, and warfare,
and labour; but it will be a noble life, a useful life,
and when the work is over there comes rest. My
choice is made. So he took Virtue by the hand,
and asked her to be his guide, and to lead him to
his work and to his labour unto the evening.

Well, Hercules set forth to do his duty, and to
help others. He did many wonderful things, about
which I have not time to tell you now. Sometimes
he delivered a country from wild beasts, at other
times he set a king free from his enemies. After a
time this strong hero came under the power of a
very mighty and very cruel king, who was jealous of
him, and wished him to lose his place in the
Heavens. For a time Hercules was obliged to do
whatever tasks this king set him, so he undertook
twelve labours, some of which seemed quite impossible. The king gave him these hard things to
do, hoping that he might fail, and perish in trying.
But the Powers, which the Greeks called gods,
favoured him, and gave him precious gifts. Minerva,
the goddess of *Wisdom*, gave him a coat of armour
and a helmet. Mercury gave him a sword, another
presented him with a shield, and in addition they
armed him with a bow and arrow, and a club of

brass. Thus armed Hercules began his labours, of which I am only going to mention a few. His first task was to kill a terrible lion, the terror of all the country round. When his roar was heard, men trembled, and women seized their children and fled shrieking. When the lion came down on the villages and farms, he would carry off cattle, and sometimes men, women and children, and no one dared to interfere with him. You can fancy, children, what a hard task it was that Hercules had to do. The king felt sure that he would fail. Well, Hercules went to meet the lion, and shot at him from a distance with his bow and arrow. But the darts were broken against the lion's thick hide, without doing him any hurt. Then the strong man drew near and attacked him with his club. But although he drove the lion back, he could not wound him. At last Hercules pursued him right into his den, and there stood the savage beast growling at him in the darkness. Then Hercules went close to him and seized him by the throat, and after a fierce fight he choked him to death. The king was so frightened at seeing Hercules return, wearing the lion's skin, that he would not suffer him to enter the city, and for a time set him no task. After awhile the king gave the strong man another very difficult labour to

perform. This was to kill a frightful monster called
the Hydra, which had a hundred heads. Hercules
did battle with this monster as boldly as he had
done with the lion, but he found whenever he cut
off one of its heads, two others grew in the place of
it. At first he thought that he should never
conquer the Hydra, but he discovered after a time
that he must burn the wound which he had made,
with fire, and then the heads would not grow. So
after a very long and fierce struggle, the Hydra was
destroyed. Another of the tasks which the king
set Hercules to do was to clean the stables of
Augeas, in which three thousand cattle had been
kept for years, and which had never been cleansed.
Many other wonderful things were done by the
strong man, but I have not time to speak of them.
Strong and brave as he was, Hercules once fell into
great weakness and sin. He went to live in the
palace of a certain Queen, and here he forgot all
about his duty and his courage, and became so
weak and womanish that they dressed him in
woman's clothes and set him to spin, whilst they
mocked him. But he repented of his folly and
weakness, and departed to other labours, till the
time came for him to find rest.

And now let us look at the lessons which this

story teaches us. First of all, do you remember anyone mentioned in the Bible who was very strong, and did many mighty works? Yes, Samson, and you will see that the history of Samson and the story of Hercules are very much alike. Both killed a lion, both lost their strength by falling into the hands of a wicked woman. No doubt the Greeks got their story of Hercules from the Jewish history of Samson.

When you were baptised, you were signed with the sign of the Cross. Why? To show that here-after you must not be ashamed to confess the faith of Christ crucified. And more than that, to show that you must fight manfully under His banner of the Cross, and continue Christ's soldiers and servants unto your life's end. So you see that being a Christian means *fighting*. Hercules had to go through all sorts of dangers before he found rest ; and we must struggle, and fight, and overcome, before we can enter the rest which remains for the people of God. There is a text about that in the Book of Revelation—"He that overcometh shall inherit all things." Now Hercules, you know, was very strong. Are we strong? are you little children very strong? No, and yet we are strong enough to do what God requires of us. Jesus says, "My strength is sufficient for thee." We have "no power of ourselves to help ourselves," but God gives us that power. Can you tell how, or when? In Holy Baptism the Holy Spirit comes to us and makes us begin to grow strong. In Confirmation the same Holy Spirit comes to a young boy or girl just growing up, and makes them strong. In the blessed Sacrament of Holy Communion we are made strong. When we ask for help earnestly in prayer we are made strong. You remember that the first trouble which came upon Hercules came when he was quite a little child. Two serpents came to attack him That teaches us that very little children can be tempted as well as grown people. Who is the serpent who attacks us? That old serpent the devil. He tempts children to be disobedient, and obstinate, and passionate, and idle, to tell lies, and take things which do not belong to them. Hercules, you remember, seized the serpents and crushed them to death. Our lesson is that we must fight with temptation. God will help us to conquer sin, if we fight against it. You must try to be good children, and ask God to help you. You cannot be good without God, and God will not make you good unless you wish to be, and try to be. When a bad thought comes into your mind, or an angry word springs to your lips, think—*there comes the serpent to hurt me.* Then say a little prayer, "Jesu, help Thy child, keep me from the tempter's power." Then try hard to get away from the bad thought, or to choke down the angry word. And do the same with all your temptations. If you see something belonging to another, and you are tempted to take it, then stop, and think—*the serpent is coming,* if I do this I shall be a thief! Then pray, "Lord, keep my hands from picking and stealing; give me strength to meet temptation."

But I must not say more to-day. We have learnt that we must fight with sin, and work out our own salvation before we can enter Paradise. We have seen that God gives us all needful strength, and that, even as little children, we have a battle to fight, and that even little children who pray are strong enough to crush down Satan under their feet.

SERMON IX.

THE STRONG MAN. (II.)

REVELATION XXI. 7.

"He that overcometh shall inherit all things."

YOU will remember, children, that I was telling you lately about Hercules, and that I tried to show you some lessons springing from the strong man's story. You will remember too, that when Hercules was growing up into a young man, he had a choice to make. He had to decide whether he would make duty, or sinful pleasure his guide.

You have the same choice to make, over and over again you are called upon to decide whether you will choose your own way, or the way of duty.

When a soldier is encamped on the battle-field, he would *like* to sleep comfortably in his tent, but presently the bugle sounds, and his *duty* calls him to spring up, and grip his weapons, and fight. The sailor would prefer the comforts of home, and the safety of the land, but his duty takes him to sea, and he must not mind the storm, and the dark nights, and the tossing waves, he has his duty to do. You have all heard of Lord Nelson, the great sailor. Well, when he was going to fight a famous battle, he sent a message to every ship in the fleet. You know that ships at sea talk to each other by means of flags, which mean certain words. When the fleet saw the flags flying from the Admiral's ship, just before the battle, every one looked eagerly to see what the message was, and it was this,—" England expects that every man will this day do his duty."

God expects that every one of His servants, men, women, and children, will do their duty. There are two kinds of duty which you have to do : your duty towards God, and your duty towards your neighbour, you can tell me what they are in the words in the Catechism.

Now, remember that the devil will tempt you away from your duty. He will tell you that it is so hard to do right, that the path of duty is a difficult one

to walk in.   Don't listen to the tempter.   You must
make your choice.   You must say to yourselves—
which shall I do, *what I like*, or *what I ought?*
Then ask God to help you, and determine " by God's
grace I will do my duty, even Jesus Christ pleased
not Himself."

Next, you remember that the strong man fell into
the power of a very wicked king, who was jealous of
him.   Well, Satan the prince of darkness, is jealous
of us.   He was an angel in Heaven once, and he is
jealous of us because Heaven has been promised to
us hereafter.   Just as the king in the story set Hercules
to fight against the lion, and the hydra, and many
other foes, Satan sends us all kinds of enemies,
temptations, which we must conquer, or they will
destroy us.   The strong man was provided with
armour and weapons, let us think about our armour.
"Take unto you the whole armour of God, that you
may be able to stand against the wiles of the devil."
And that armour is not what you have seen in
pictures, and which soldiers used to wear in the old
days.   You know that a steel breast-plate would not
keep out a bad thought, nor would a sword of steel
strike down the tempter.   Our enemies are Spiritual,
so our armour must be Spiritual also.   Can you
remember, children, the names of the whole armour

of God? What must we have for a girdle? Truth.
Yes, and to guard our heart we must wear the breast-
plate of righteousness; and our feet must be shod
with the Gospel, that means, we must stand firm on
the Gospel promises. Then our head will need a
defence, so we must have the helmet of salvation,
and to cover and guard ourselves we should take the
shield of Faith. And what is our sword? The
sword of the Spirit, the help of God the Holy Ghost.
When you pray earnestly, that sword is put into
your hand. When you are confirmed that sword is
put into your hand.

In former times, it was often the custom for an
old warrior, who had gained many victories, to give
his sword to his son, and bid him use it bravely as his
father had done. So God, our Father, gives us the
sword of the Spirit, and says to each of us, " quit
you like men, and fight." Hercules had to fight
with a lion. Our enemy, the devil, as a roaring lion
goeth about, seeking whom he may devour. He comes
down on the sheep-fold—the Church, and he tries to
seize the lambs—the children of the flock. When
you find a child using bad words, laughing at religion,
never praying, or reading his Bible, you know at
once what it means. *The lion has got him.* He has
carried that child off to his dark den of sin. When

you see that you must try to help him, pray for him, talk to him, and try to get him to do better, that's the way to deliver him from the lion's den.

My children, when you sin wilfully the lion has got hold of you. If you tell a lie, you are in the lion's den. If you are disobedient to parents or teachers, if you are in a passion, you are in the lion's den. If you were to go to a menagerie, or wild beast show, and if, by some accident, you got into the cage with the lion, would you not be terribly frightened? Would it not be very dreadful to see his fierce glaring eyes, and cruel teeth, and to hear his deep roar of anger? Yes, but it is far more awful to fall into the power of the devil. The lion can only hurt your body; Satan can destroy your soul. Hercules fought with the lion, so must we fight with our lion. "Resist the devil and he will flee from thee." You remember how the strong man began his battle with the lion. He shot arrows at him from a distance, and they had no effect. Sometime we keep a long way off from our sins, and *wish*. We say, "Oh, I *wish* I were better. I *wish* I could conquer my temper, or I wish I did not make my mother so unhappy." Wishing won't help you, my children. You are like Hercules, shooting your arrows from a distance. You mustget close to the lion, and struggle with it. You must get hold of your sin, and see how bad and ugly it is, and then you must fight with it, grapple with it, crying out to Jesus, "I am weak, but Thou art mighty, hold me in Thy powerful hand, help me *now*."

Next, the strong man had to fight with a monster, having a hundred heads. I wonder what that teaches us? Surely, that Satan sends us temptations in a hundred different forms. Sin is a monster with hundred heads, very ugly heads too, and each has a sting in it. All the strong man's fighting could not destroy the monster, till he was helped by *fire*.

That teaches us this lesson. That all our struggles with sin are useless, unless the Holy Spirit is with us to help. The Holy Spirit is often spoken of in the Bible as a Fire, and it is that fire which alone can destroy the power of sin, only we must do our part, and fight.

I told you that one of the tasks which Hercules had to perform was to clean out the stables of Angeas. I think we have all such a task to do daily. We have to look into our lives, and see what bad thoughts and wishes are hiding there, and then, by God's help, we must try to get rid of them. Do you know that the Chinese have a very wise saying, "The best way to keep the city clean, is for every

one to sweep before his own door." Remember
that, children ; don't think about the faults of others,
but about your own ; and *sweep before your own door*.

Now think, what is my sin, my special temptation?
Am I fighting against it as hard as I can ?   Cannot
I pray more often, and more earnestly? cannot I keep
a more strict watch over my words ?

Then think of the hydra—the hideous monster
sin, with its hundred heads. The devil sends us temptations in many different forms. For one, there is bad
company ; for another, there is a vile book ; for some
there is a passionate, unruly temper; for others, there
is pride, which teaches a child to be sulky when he
is reproved, and to mutter to himself, "I don't care."
And there are hundreds of other temptations.   Be
prepared for them, they come from your enemy, the
devil.   Ask Jesus who was tempted to help you in
temptation.   Say to Him, "Lord, I am weak, I am
only a little tempted child, help me to fight, and
to triumph against the world, and the flesh, and the
devil."

SERMON X.

THE BEAUTIFUL GARDEN

ROMANS V. 12.

"By one man sin entered into the world, and death by sin."

ONCE upon a time, long ago, so the old Greeks tell us, there was a very beautiful garden. It must have been better than any which we have ever seen, for nothing in it grew old, or ever died; the flowers were always blooming, and the fruit was ever ripe. There were no venomous reptiles nor insects in the garden, no black clouds to darken the sky, no storms, nor blight, nor frost. A number of children lived and played in this beautiful garden: at least, they seemed like children, for they never grew old. They were perfectly innocent and happy, and never

E

tired. They knew nothing about pain or trouble; they had never heard of head-ache, or tooth-ache, or medicine, and they didn't know what tears and crying meant. Moreover, these children never quarrelled with each other; you never saw them with red faces, and flashing eyes, and doubled fists. They never struck or pinched each other, or said cross, unkind words. No child was jealous of another, for everyone loved everyone else. You can see that this must have been a very long time ago, when the world was quite young.

Well, among the children was a boy, who lived with his companion in a little cottage in the beautiful garden, all covered over with climbing flowers. The girl's name was Pandora, and the way in which she got her name was this : the Greeks fancied that all their gods had given her gifts; one had given her beauty, another cleverness, one sent the gift of singing, another of dancing; so she was called Pandora, which means *every gift*. These children were perfectly happy, like the others in the beautiful garden. They had no cares or anxieties ; they were never doubtful about to-morrow, but when it came it was as happy as the day before. One day, however, when Pandora entered their cottage, she saw a mysterious-looking box in one corner. She

asked how it had come there, and her companion
told her that it had been brought by a stranger, and
that the stranger had bidden him take great care of
the box, and if he would be happy, and make others
so, he must on no account open the lid. Soon a
change came over Pandora, she was not so perfectly
happy and gay as she had been. The mysterious
box was always in her mind; she was continually
looking at it, and wondering what it held. Instead
of wandering through the beautiful garden with
her companion, gathering the flowers which never
faded, Pandora stayed in the cottage, looking at the
box. Sometimes she fancied she could hear
whispering voices around her. What *could* be in
the box? She asked the question over and over
again. Then she thought there could be no harm
in opening the lid, and she talked to her brother
about it; but he reminded her that they were
forbidden to do so, if they would be happy themselves, and make others so. Then he would ask
Pandora to come and play with him as of old, but
she seemed to care no longer for the garden and
its pleasures, and sat in the cottage looking at the
box. And so the cottage was not so happy and full
of sunshine as before, when Pandora had been
perfectly content. Every day, as she fixed her

longing eyes on the box, she seemed to hear a whisper in her ear—"Open the lid a little way, it can't do any harm."

Now of course it was a very great temptation for Pandora. Would not you have wanted very much to open the lid? It was very natural that Pandora should wish to know what was in the box, but she should have remembered the command and have kept away from the temptation. Instead of that she always had the box before her eyes, and sometimes she would try to lift it, but it was far too heavy, and fastened with strongly knotted cords.

One day Pandora thought to herself that there could be no harm in unfastening the knotted cord, she need not touch the lid. She was alone in the cottage, her brother was playing with other children in the beautiful garden, and Pandora could hear through the open window the sounds of singing birds and merry voices. But her face was very anxious and troubled, as her fingers were busy with the knots in the cord. Why did not she hasten away, and seek her brother, and join in his play? No, the voice kept whispering in her ear—"It won't do any harm!" Still she handled the knot, till suddenly it became unfastened. Then Pandora was frightened at what she had done. She tried with trembling fingers to tie the cord again, but although it was easy to unfasten the knot, it was impossible for her to tie it again. She placed one hand on the lid of the box: the voice was whispering very loudly now—"Lift it just a little, it won't matter!" Whilst she hesitated, her brother entered the cottage, just in time to see Pandora raise the lid. Then a very wonderful thing happened. A black cloud, like smoke, rushed out of the box, nearly choking the children. This cloud seemed crowded with living creatures, all struggling together, and it soon filled the cottage, once so bright and clean, and made it black and dirty. The window of the cottage was open, and the cloud rolled out of it, and spread all over the beautiful garden, till the sunshine was quite hidden. Pandora was so frightened that she shut down the lid of the box and stood crying. She had never cried before, had never known what tears meant. What had she done? She did not know. People who do wrong, my children, never know how much harm they have caused. But what had Pandora done? The mysterious box held all the troubles of the world; all the diseases, and aches, and pains, and sorrows, and cares; all the bad tempers and angry passions, and Pandora had let them out.

Now the beautiful garden was changed. Dark clouds and thick fogs hid the sunshine, and the flowers drooped and withered. ₁The fruit was blighted, and the children were no longer the happy, gay creatures they had been. They began to grow old; they no longer cared for innocent play, for they had all sorts of troubles to bear. One had a head-ache, another was tired, this one found fault with his food, that one ate of it too greedily. Instead of the happy songs and laughter which used to be heard in the garden, angry voices and quarrelling disturbed the once peaceful scene. The leaves fell from the trees, and withered. The children became old and feeble, and died, and were no more seen. What had been the beautiful garden became almost like a desert. Pandora and her brother were very sad and miserable, but that would not undo the mischief.

Presently Pandora, thinking that nothing now remained in the box, raised the lid again, and immediately a bright star seemed to rise out of the chest, and shine above them. Whilst the children gazed on the star, and felt comforted, a voice told them that it was called *Hope*, and then when all the troubles were let loose among men, Hope remained to them.

So Pandora and her brother went forth from the once happy cottage, ruined by disobedience ; and instead of playing in the beautiful garden, they went far away into a strange country, where they had to work hard every day. They felt, too, that they were daily growing older, and they often felt pain, and shed many tears. But then they looked up, and saw the Star of Hope shining, and so they took courage. They had been promised that Hope should lead them on, till at last they should find the beautiful garden again, fair as ever, with no fading flower, no sorrow, nor crying.

Now, my children, let us turn from the parable, and learn its lessons. The beautiful garden reminds us of Paradise, when all the world was young, and fresh, and fair; when God looked on all that He had made, "and behold, it was very good"; when there were no troubles, nor sorrows, because there was no sin. When we hear of Pandora having all the gifts of the gods, we think of Eve, fresh from the hands of God, and dwelling in the beautiful garden of Eden. There came a whisper of temptation to Pandora to be disobedient; so, too, the tempter spoke to Eve, and said, "Ye shall not surely die." I told you how Pandora kept looking at the box, and at last opened the lid. So Eve began by looking at the forbidden fruit, and wishing for it, and ended by tasting it.

My children, when a temptation comes to you look away from it; if you are tempted to look, you will be tempted to wish, and wishing will be followed by doing what is wrong. What were the sins of Pandora? Curiosity and disobedience. Yes, and these were the very sins of Eve. Well, after Pandora had been disobedient, and had opened the box, all the world was filled with sorrow, and sins, and sicknesses. People had to work in pain and trouble; they began to grow old, and die. Not only were Pandora and her brother punished, but everyone suffered for her sin. Can you remember a text which tells us how sin and death came into the world? "By one man sin entered into the world, and death by sin, and so death passed upon all men, for all have sinned." You rememember that after Pandora had sinned the people in the beautiful garden were all changed, they began to quarrel with each other. That reminds us that after Adam and Eve fell Cain hated his brother Abel, and slew him.

My children, as long as you keep innocency, and try to do the will of Jesus, and keep close to Him, you are, as it were, living in Paradise. Innocency is like that beautiful garden of Eden. But when you do wrong, when you do what God has forbidden, all becomes changed, you are no more happy, innocent children, you are like Pandora when she had raised the lid of her fatal box. Troubles and sorrows are around you, and they are the fruits of sin. You are not only unhappy yourselves, but you make others so; a bad child makes others miserable. Every time you get into a passion, or tell a lie, or do some other wrong thing, you are like Pandora opening the box of troubles.

But although the child in the parable had done wrong, and was punished, something was sent to comfort her—the Star of Hope. Was there any such Star of Hope given to Adam and Eve? Yes, indeed, although their sin brought sorrow, and death on all men, there was given the promise of a Saviour, of Jesus, the Bright and Morning Star. They and all men were to live in the hope of a Redeemer, who should conquer sin and death. Do you remember how certain men, mentioned in the Gospel, did see the Star of Hope guiding them? Yes, the Wise Men from the East; and "when they saw the star, they rejoiced with exceeding great joy." We have lost the beautiful garden of Paradise through Adam's sin, and we all have to work in this world, and to bear sorrow and pain, but every Christian child can look on the Star of Hope, guiding him to Jesus.

Let our prayer be this :—"Grant us, we beseech Thee, that having this hope, we may purify ourselves even as He is pure ; that when He shall appear again, with power and great glory, we may be made like unto Him in His eternal and glorious kingdom."

SERMON XI.

THE NEW WORLD

REVELATION XXI. I.

"I saw a new Heaven, and a new earth."

HAVE you ever seen a shell brought from the bottom of the sea? It has been lying there among the coral, and the bright sea-weeds, perhaps for many, many years. The fish, whose house the shell once was, has been dead for a long time, and the shell lies in your hand quite still and silent. But if you put it close to your ear you will find that the shell is not silent, it makes a sound like the winds and waves. For ages, perhaps, the sea has been telling its wonderful story to the shell, down in the deep

clear water, and I like to fancy that when we listen
to it the shell repeats the story to us. Ah! what
marvellous stories, and what wonderful secrets the
sea must have.

Perhaps you have heard of the little dying boy,
who, when he sat on the shore, and watched the
waves rolling in, one after another, wanted to know
what they were saying. It would be very delightful,
children, if we could only understand what "the
wild waves are saying." Well, let us fancy that we
are holding the shell to our ear, and listening to the
story of the sea, what will it tell us? what will it teach
us? There are so many stories for the shell to tell
us. One is about storms and tempest, when the
good ship was broken and battered by the waves;
another story is about poor ship-wrecked people, who
have drifted for days in an open boat, without food,
or water, suffering terrible pain, but saved at last by
God's mercy. There are many such sad stories
which the shell could tell us. Or it might be a
story of a battle fought at sea; how once a great
fleet came to attack England, called the Invincible
Armada, and how brave British sailors went forth to
meet the Spaniard, and how the fleet was all broken
and destroyed. Or the shell might whisper the story
of Augustine and his monks. It might tell us how,

long ago, when the Saxons ruled in England, and when princes and people were heathens, and worshipped idols, forty holy men landed in Kent, and told the Saxon king, and his fierce warriors, about Jesus, the meek and gentle. A beautiful story is that, my children, how our forefathers became Christians, and how the Cathedral of Canterbury was built, and another ancient Church there, where you may see, as I have seen, the very font in which the Saxon Queen was baptized. But these are not the stories which the sea-shell will tell us now. This shell came, perhaps, from the deep blue ocean which rolls around the West Indian Islands, and it will murmur to us about lovely spots where palm-trees grow, and the most delicious fruits hang on the trees, and the birds and flowers are of the brightest and most beautiful colours. But the shell will tell us more; it will tell us the story of the man who discovered those lovely places, the New World, as they were called. This is the story.

Close upon four hundred years ago, there was living a great and brave man, named Christopher Columbus. Each of his two names has a very important meaning. Christopher signifies, *Christbearer;* and Columbus means *a dove.* So this great and brave sailor was *the Christ-bearing dove.* A very

beautiful name, my children, and he was worthy of
it. Wherever he went he bore the love of Christ
in his heart, and although he was as brave as a lion,
yet he was as gentle and patient as a dove. ● In the
times when Columbus lived people were very
ignorant. Any of you children would be astonished
at the little they knew. But you must remember
that there were very few schools, very few books,
and very few people who could read and write. In
Spain, where Columbus was living, the king and the
queen, as well as the most learned scholars, believed
that the world was flat instead of round. Well
Columbus, who was much wiser than they, and had
often been to sea, assured the king that the world
was round, and that there were other lands far off,
rich and beautiful, if only they could be found.
Some people laughed at Columbus, and thought
him mad; others tried to dissuade him from seeking
the New World. Every one put difficulties in his
way, but he persevered, though he was persecuted,
and insulted, and disappointed, over and over
again. He felt that God had chosen him to discover
this New World, and to be the *Christ-bearer* to those
who had never heard of Jesus. At last, after a very
long time, Columbus managed to get some ships
and men, and set sail. I have not time to tell you

about his trials and misfortunes; how some of the sailors mutinied, and tried to throw their captain overboard; how they cried like cowards at the sight of the wide, unknown ocean, how they actually thought, in their ignorance, that the ship would sail to the edge of the flat world, and then fall over it. The crew tried to force Columbus to go back, but he sailed steadily on, day after day, praying to God that he might find the New World, bearing the love of Christ in his heart.

One day some strange birds flew round his ship, then a branch covered with berries floated by, and Columbus knew he was near land. Presently they saw the shore, and all fell on their knees and thanked God that they had discovered the New World. Then Columbus landed, and holding up the cross, took possession in the name of Christ, and called the island San Salvador, which means *Holy Saviour*.

Well, after this, Columbus found many other lands, and bore many sorrows and misfortunes. He was cruelly ill-treated, and at one time loaded with chains, and he died poor and neglected; but he had done his duty, and was able with his last breath to thank God that he had found the New World.

This is the sea-shell's story of Christopher Columbus. I think, my children, we may find a lesson here. First, the name of the great discoverer should teach us something. He was called Christopher—the *Christ-bearer*. Now you all have a Christian name, which is given you in your Baptism, and although, perhaps, none of you were baptised Christopher, yet in one sense you are all *Christ-bearers*. Every Christian child is pledged to bear something—the *name of Christ*, and to be made like unto Him. Yes, and more than that, every Christian must *bear his Cross*, for Jesus says if any man will be His disciple, he must take up his cross, and follow Him. What does bearing the cross mean, my children? Denying ourselves, giving up our own way, bearing trouble and sorrow patiently. Yes, it means all this, and it means, too, putting up with other people's tempers and unkindness, being meek and forgiving when people say cruel and unjust things about us. O, my children, everyone of you should try to be a Christopher,—a *Christ-bearer*.

Then the second name of the great discoverer means a *Dove*. Every true Christian should be *gentle*. Our Lord says, "Be ye wise as serpents, and harmless as doves." It is not a sign of courage to be rough, and violent, and cruel. The bravest and most famous men have been gentle. Columbus was a hero, yet he was well named the Christ-bearing dove. To be gentle, patient, self-denying, is a sure mark of a brave man, and of a Christian man also. The great wish of Columbus was to discover the New World. That also should be the great desire of our life. Do you know where that New World is? In Heaven,—the better country, that is a Heavenly. We know there is such a New World. Our Lord says, " In My Father's house are many mansions, I go to prepare a place for you." And S. John tells us that in his wonderful vision he saw "a new Heaven, and a new earth." Ignorant people laughed at Columbus, and told him there was no New World, and tried to keep him back from seeking it. There are such people now, some ignorant, some wicked, who try to make us believe that when we leave this world there is no new world for us to go to. You would not like to think that, my children. You would not like to believe that your dear mother who is gone, or your little brother, or sister, who left the earth, have no home now, and that you never will see them again. You would rather believe with me, that we have a home eternal in the Heavens.

Well, you remember that Columbus had to cross many waters, and to bear many sorrows and troubles

F

before he found the New World. We have to do
the same. Before we begin our journey to the New
World, we must pass through the water of Baptism,
then we set out on the road to Heaven, the narrow
way which leads to life eternal. Every time you try
to do right, and to conquer sin; every time you
come near to God in prayer, and in the services of
the Church ; every time you elder children come to
the Altar in Holy Communion, you have got a step
nearer the New World. And there are other waters
to be crossed, dark waters of temptation, bitter storms
of sorrow or self-denial, rough waves of difficulty,—
the waves of this troublesome world. But just as
God brought Columbus safe through all, so the same
God will carry you, His children, you who are called
to be in character, Christ-bearing doves, through all
trials, and bring you safe through all temptations ;
and when you have passed through the last sea of
all, which is called *death*, your eyes shall look on the
beauty of the New World, and "so shall you be
ever with the Lord."

Once a little sickly boy was taken by kind friends
from a stifling London garret, for a pleasure trip in
a river steamer. As he looked at the crowd of ships
lying around him, preparing for their voyage, he
asked where they were all going. He was told that

they were going abroad. After a long silence, he raised his eyes up towards the blue sky, and whispered, "I am going abroad too," and so passed away to the New World, the better country, "the land beyond the sea."

SERMON XII.

THE STRANGE GUESTS.

HEBREWS XIII. 2.

"Be not forgetful to entertain strangers: for thereby some
have entertained angels unawares."

LISTEN to another story of the old Greeks, which
carries a very beautiful lesson with it. You
remember that these Greeks did not know the true
God, and worshipped all sorts of false gods. Well,
they tell us that the people in a certain part of the
world had become very rich, and very wicked. They
were specially cruel to strangers, and if any traveller
visited their neighbourhood they would drive him
from their doors, and often stone him with stones.
Things grew so bad, that at last two of the gods,

as the Greeks called them, determined to come on the earth in human form, and judge for themselves. They took the shape of poor, roughly-clad travellers, and went from one great house to another, asking for food and shelter. Now if the people who lived in those grand houses had known who the travellers were, they would have opened the doors gladly, and have given them of their best. But they only saw two poor way-faring men, who asked for a little food, and a night's lodging; so the cruel people of the town drove them away, and even threw stones at them. At last, when the two travellers had been driven quite outside the city, they saw a simple thatched cottage, standing on the hill-side. It did not seem very likely that they would find any refreshment there, for the place evidently belonged to poor people. But we must never judge by *appearances*, my children. The people of this cottage *were* very poor, but they were good, and kind and honest, not the least like the other dwellers in the town

The owner of the cottage was an old man named Philemon, who tilled a little patch of ground, and managed to live honestly, but very poorly. Both he and his old wife Baucis were ashamed of their wicked neighbours in the town, and were always ready to show kindness to strangers. · The two travellers went to the cottage door, and asked for food, and lodging. Instead of shutting the door against them, or calling them bad names, as the people in the town had done, Baucis and Philemon made the strangers welcome. They set such common food as they had before them, and a cup of wine, the only one remaining. The travellers sat down to their meal, and told the old cottagers that they could afford to pay for their food. But Baucis and Philemon would take no money, and assured their guests that they were welcome to such as they had. Then the strange guests asked the old people to sup with them, but they declined, because there was little enough for the travellers, and nothing more in the house.

One of the strangers, however, spoke as one in authority, and said, " Fear not, Baucis and Philemon, the food shall not fail." So the old people sat down to the table, and although the supper was the same coarse fare which they always had, it now tasted like the most delicious food which ever was served in a rich man's house.

Baucis and Philemon looked on their guests, and on each other, with astonishment, and presently they had still more reason to do so. They had noticed that the cup of wine, the only wine in the cottage, had been emptied. Yet when the two travellers passed the cup to Philemon it was full to the brim, and the wine was such as no man, not even the most wealthy, had ever tasted. And when at last supper was ended, there was just as much food and wine as when they commenced the meal. Whilst the old cottagers were wondering what these things might mean, the strange guests told them that they had entertained no common travellers; and that as a reward for their unselfish kindness, they should never be in want, or poverty.

Then the strangers asked Baucis and Philemon to guide them to the top of the hill. When they had reached the summit, they turned to look back at the town, which lay in a valley. But there was no town to be seen. The old people shaded their eyes, and looked anxiously for the well-known streets and houses, but they could see nothing but a great lake of water, which filled the whole valley. The wicked town was drowned. Only one house was to be seen, and that was the thatched cottage of Philemon. Again, the old people looked sadly at the lake, for they pitied their wicked neighbours, who had been so terribly punished. But when they turned their eyes once more to their own cottage, that too had disappeared, and in its place stood a beautiful temple, with fair marble columns shining in the setting sunlight.

Then the strange guests told Baucis and Philemon that this was their future home, and that they should live in the beautiful temple, and tend and keep it. "And now," said the travellers, "we must leave you, but, before we go, ask what you will, and you shall have your wish, in return for the kindness you have shown." So Baucis and Philemon, who were simple, contented folks, and had no thought of riches or honour, asked that, as they had lived so long together, and grown old side by side, they might both die on the same day, so that in death they might not be parted. Their request was granted; and when, many years afterwards, the two old people died in the same hour, travellers noticed two fair trees, an oak and a lime, standing over their graves, beneath whose shade the weary wayfarer loved to rest, and tell the story of Baucis and Philemon.

Now, my children, this old story of the Greeks is a parable for us to learn from. It teaches us one very plain lesson, to be unselfish, to think of others, to help our neighbour. Our Saviour, Jesus, taught the same lesson, in the parable of the Good Samaritan. You see those humble cottagers were

entertaining very great people indeed, although they
did not know it. There is a text in the Bible which
says something about this. "Be not forgetful to
entertain strangers, for thereby some have entertained angels unawares." Can you remember
anyone mentioned in the Bible who thus entertained
angels unawares? Abraham, when he dwelt in the
plains of Mamre. And Lot, also, when he was sitting
in the gate of wicked Sodom, was visited by two
angels. When those two strange visitors came to
Baucis and Philemon, you remember that the store
of food and wine did not fail. Now that is only a
legend; but there is a true story in the Bible of a
poor widow who entertained God's prophet, Elijah,
and her barrel of meal, and her cruse of oil, were
supplied by a miracle. Thus we learn that if we are
good and kind to others, God will reward us, and
not let us come to want.

And now let us learn another lesson. Was there
not someone else who came down to this earth, and
lived poor and despised among men? Yes, you
know that the Lord Jesus Christ, the only Begotten
Son of God, became man, and dwelt among us.
He went to many homes, and said, "Behold I
stand at the door, and knock." And they would
not open to Him. Some few made Jesus

welcome, like Martha and Mary, and the disciples, but most people despised Him, and tried to kill Him: Now think, dear children, does Jesus Christ ever come to our homes now, and knock at the door? Yes, in one sense He does. He comes to us, and offers to abide with us, and bless us. Do you know *how* He lives with us? In our hearts. I wonder whether you know how we can open the door to Jesus Christ, so that He may come in and dwell with us? I will tell you; whenever you do anything good or loving to one of Christ's people, you do it to Christ Himself. He says, "Inasmuch as ye have done it unto one of the least of these, my brethren, ye have done it unto Me." I will tell you a story about that. Long ago, there was a brave soldier, named Martin, who, though not yet baptized, desired to become a Christian, and was being prepared for the holy rite. One day, when Martin was riding forth from a French town with his brother officers, a poor, half-naked beggar lay at the city gate, shivering with cold, and asked for alms. The other soldiers rode by without heeding him, but Martin drew his sword, and cutting his soldier's cloak in half, gave the one part to cover the beggar. Martin's companions laughed at him as he rode along with half a cloak; but that night, when he had gone to bed, a vision appeared to Martin, and he thought he saw the Lord Jesus wrapped in a garment which he knew. As the vision grew brighter, Martin saw that the Saviour was wearing the very half of the cloak which he had given to the beggar.

And now one thought more. When the Lord Jesus comes to dwell with us, and be our guest, He promises us such good things as pass man's understanding. He says, "Behold I stand at the door, and knock; if any man hear My voice, and open the door, I will come in to him, and will sup with him, and he with Me." Yes, my children, if Jesus be our guest, He will give us food which never fails, and you know that that food is the Bread of Heaven, the Blessed Sacrament of Christ's Body and Blood. And He will grant unto us not to die all at one time, but to live for ever; for He has promised, "Whosoever liveth and believeth in Me, shall never die." Dear children, if your hearts are full of love for Jesus, and for each other, He will come and dwell there. Let us sing to Him to-day :—

> " Thou didst leave Thy throne and Thy kingly crown,
>   When Thou camest to earth for me ;
> But in Bethlehem's home was there found no room
>   For Thy Holy Nativity.
> Oh ! come to my heart, Lord Jesus,
> There is room in my heart for Thee."

SERMON XIII.

TWO LIVES.

S. MARK X. 14.

" Suffer the little children to come unto Me."

IN a certain city there were two little boys. They were of the same age, but one was rich and the other was poor. The rich child lived in a large house, surrounded by a beautiful garden. He had loving parents, and wise teachers, and attentive servants to wait on him, and he was happy as the day was long. The poor child lived in a garret, in a narrow back street of the city. He was not only poor, but sickly, and a cripple. He had been left an orphan, and the only relations he had thought the crippled, white-faced child a trouble to them. Very often the little boy was obliged to lie for days upon his wretched bed, too weak and ill to get up. The room where he lived was small and ugly. There was nothing to brighten it or make it cheerful, and the only window looked into the sky. In the summer the hot sun shone down from the blue sky, and made the garret stifling as an oven. In the winter the rain fell, and blurred the tiny window, as if with tears. Day after day, in the summer time, the poor crippled child lay in this hot room. He heard the merry voices of other children in the street, and knew that they were going forth to play in pleasant meadows outside the town. How he longed to go with them, to run in the cricket field, or to roll amid the hay, or to gather flowers in the hedgerows ! When he heard the Church bells chiming from many a steeple, the poor crippled boy thought of the healthy, happy children, who were going to sing in the choir, and to praise Jesus, the children's Friend. .And then, though he felt very lonely, he took comfort, for he remembered that a good man had told him how his Guardian Angel was always watching over him, in his poor, hot garret-room. One day, when the little boy had managed to crawl downstairs, he saw that some of

his neighbours had been moving from the narrow
street. There was a litter of straw and rubbish
lying in the road, and old, worn out articles which
had been thrown away as useless. Among them
there was a flower-pot, old and cracked, and in it
was growing a common wild flower, which some
child had brought home from the fields. ·The poor,
weakly boy, who could not go to the meadows,
looked on the flower as a thing of beauty. Its
yellow blossoms seemed to him like gold. The old
cracked flower pot was as precious in his eyes as the
rich man's conservatory. Tenderly he carried the
wild flower to his garret, and watered it daily with
loving hands. It seemed to him, as he watched it,
that the poor, common weed had the power to carry
him out into the country. He could almost believe
that he was lying among the soft, sweet grass,
listening to the bird's song, or gathering great
bunches of primroses, or resting beneath the shadow
of some tall tree The narrow, ugly walls of his
garret seemed to open, and he could look out, not
on the hot dusty city street, but over green hills,
and meadows all dotted with flowers. But soon the
poor field-flower withered and died in the stifling
garret, and then the little boy saw no more visions
of the country.

At last, one day, the crippled child was able to walk very slowly, and with much pain, outside the city streets, and he came to the gate of a large and beautiful garden. He pressed his thin white face to the iron bars of the gate, and knew that he had never seen anything half so beautiful before. There were smooth lawns of soft grass, where fountains threw up their spray, and bubbled into basins for gold and silver fish. Great trees threw their pleasant shade over some parts of the garden, and in others flowers of every colour filled the air with sweetness. The little white-faced cripple thought that the garden of Eden, of which he had read, must have been just like this.

There was a little boy playing in the garden, plucking a flower to pieces, and scattering its petals in the air. This was the rich man's child of whom I told you, and who knew nothing of the sorrows of the poor cripple in the garret. Presently the servants, who had noticed the white-faced, ragged child at the gate, went to him, and told him to go away. Then the tears fell fast on the orphan boy's thin cheeks, he was not to look any more on the one scene of beauty he had ever found. As he turned sadly away, the little boy in the garden caught sight of his tearful looks. He thought how different his lot

from mine ! .He is poor, and crippled, and cries at
the sight of a flower. I am rich, and strong, and
have as many flowers as I want. So the rich child
ran to a rose tree, his favourite plant, and plucked
a branch of sweet, red roses, and gave them to the
poor child at the gate. When the crippled boy
got home, his miserable room was filled with the
scent of the roses. And now it seemed to the little
boy as if those flowers had changed the whole place
for him. He did not notice that his bed was hot,
and hard, and uncomfortable. He forgot that people
often spoke harshly to him, and that no gentle hand
ever soothed his pain. As long as the roses lived
the child seemed to be in Paradise. But one after
another the flowers drooped and died, and when the
neighbours found the last rose dead, they found the
little crippled child was dead also.

About this time there was great sorrow in the
house with the beautiful garden. The child who
had played in the garden, was very ill. He would
never play there again. The best doctors came
to see him ; all that money could do was done ;
skilful nurses watched by the little boy's bed. But
in vain. One evening, when the child's mother
was praying beside his bed, the little boy saw a
shadow fall across the room, and a fair, and shining

figure stood beside him, holding out his arms.
With a little cry of pleasure, the boy stretched out
his hands. His mother started from her knees, she
saw no shadow, but she saw the child was dead.
And now the shining visitor was bearing the little
boy in his arms, through the calm, starry night, to
Paradise. And as they went upon their journey,
the Spirit looked lovingly on the child, and placed
in his hands a bunch of crimson roses. The boy
looked wonderingly at the flowers, he seemed to
have seen them before, and to know them again.
And the Spirit said softly to the child, "They are
your own roses which died, and are living again.
Do you remember how once a pale-faced, crippled
orphan stood weeping at your gate? You pitied the
lonely, suffering child, and you gave him your
favourite flowers to comfort him." And the wondering boy asked, "How do you know these things?"
And the Spirit smiled lovingly upon him, and
answered, "because I was once that crippled child.
And God has suffered me to carry you to Him,
before the world has stained you with its sin. Your
roses, the gift of love, died on earth, but they live
again in Paradise."

Learn, my children, from this parable, that no act
of love and kindness is too small to be noticed by

G

our Father in Heaven.   Every time you do a gentle,
loving deed for others, you are planting a flower in
Paradise, and you shall find it blooming, when God
calls you home.

SERMON XIV.

THE MAGIC MIRROR.

S. Matthew vil 5.

"First cast out the beam out of thine own eye; and then shalt thou see clearly to cast out the mote out of thy brother's eye."

Listen, my children, to a parable which was first told to the little children of Denmark, by one who loved them well. There was once an evil spirit, who wished to do as much mischief as possible. That is what all evil spirits desire. So he invented a glass, or mirror, which had very wonderful powers. Everything good and beautiful looked mean and ugly when seen in this mirror. The most lovely scenery looked no better than a ploughed field, and the highest mountain seemed like a mole-hill when

reflected in this glass. The fairest face of man,
woman, or child, seemed deformed and hideous
when you looked at it in the mirror, and if any one
had a spot, or freckle upon their skin, it appeared to
spread all over their face. ‚ This is what this glass
did, it made everything right look wrong, and
everything wrong seem worse. A kindly smile was
twisted by this mirror into an ugly sneer, a speck
of dust on one's clothing was magnified into a mass of
dirt. Well, the evil spirit was never tired of playing
with this mischievous glass, till one day he let it
fall, and it was broken into millions of pieces.
This was not the end of this mirror by any means,
it did more harm than ever, for all the little broken
pieces had the same power as the whole glass.
Sometimes a tiny bit of the broken mirror flew into
someone's eye, then that person saw everything, and
everybody in a wrong way. The brightest day
seemed dark, the most beautiful pictures appeared
crooked and out of drawing, the most delicate china
had a crack in it, and, worse than all, the best and
noblest actions looked selfish and mean. Sometimes
a piece of the broken glass got into a person's heart,
and then his heart became cold, and hard, and he
cared for no one but himself. Some of the glass
was made into spectacles, and the people who used

them to read with, never found anything good in their books and newspapers. If there were any bad things in the books they would see them magnified very much indeed, but all pure and noble words looked dim and indistinct through the spectacles. Some of the larger pieces of broken glass were put into windows, and whoever looked through that window never saw the face of a friend.

I have not time to tell you half the mischief which the pieces of the broken mirror did. I will tell you, however, a few of the troubles which they caused. In one busy town there were two little children, a boy and girl, who lived with their grandmother, and loved each other dearly. They liked best to play in the little garden of their home, where each had a rose tree, and they would watch every day for the first bud to open into a lovely flower. Sometimes the two children would sit side by side looking at a picture book, of which they never seemed to grow tired. Sometimes they would listen to the stories which their grandmother told them. One day the little boy felt a sharp pain in his heart, and at the same moment it seemed as though a grain of sand had flown into his eye. In a moment the child was quite changed. Two pieces of the broken looking-glass had done all the mischief. When he looked

at the rose trees it seemed as if the flowers were
blighted and worm-eaten, and he pulled up the plants
by the roots, whilst the little girl cried bitterly.
The boy was rough and rude to her, for his heart had
grown cold and hard.   The tiny speck of glass in
his eye made his sister appear ugly and cross.
When she brought the picture book, he said the
pictures were hideous, and threw it on one side.
When his grandmother told her stories he laughed
at them, and said they were only fit for babies.   If
other children asked him to play with them he was
sure to find fault, and quarrel, and accuse the others
of cheating ; in fact, the boy was quite changed, and
no one knew the reason.   It was because he had the
piece of glass in his heart and in his eye.

In another place there lived two little girls, who
had always been the best of friends.   One day
one of these children came running to see her
friend, and to show her the birthday presents which
she had received.   Just as the little girl was opening her box of treasures, the other child felt something sharp in her eye, but the minute after she felt
nothing.   The piece of glass was there, however.
And now she could see nothing to admire in her
friend's presents.   She declared that the pretty
dress was of very common stuff, and the trimming

sewn on crooked. She sneered at the little golden locket, and said it could not be real gold. And the doll, the great treasure of all, did not satisfy her, she said it was stuffed with sawdust, and had not real hair. So the little girl's birthday was spoilt, and she was never good friends with her companion any more. See what mischief a little speck of glass can do !

There were two boys living in a country village. Every Sunday they used to go to Church, and take part in the Children's Service. One Sunday the elder boy felt a sharp pain in his heart, and something flew into his eye. You know, my children, what had happened. So, instead of hastening on to Church, he proposed that they should go for a walk instead. His companion, however, refused, and got into Church just as the school children were taking their places. Well, the other boy looked at the Church, and thought to himself—what a dull, gloomy place it is ! It is much pleasanter out here. Only the Sunday before the boy had loved his Church, and had been one of the best singers among the children. But this piece of fatal glass had got into his heart, and into his eye. So on this Sunday he went skulking about the fields, till he could no longer hear the sound of the organ playing at the

Children's Service.   And by and by he came to a
farmer's orchard, and thought to himself—how ripe
and good those apples look, I never thought them
so tempting before.   He had often seen this very
orchard, but he did not covet another's goods till
this piece of glass got into his eye.   Well, it ended
in the boy being caught in the act of stealing fruit,
and he was severely punished, and lost his character.
He went on from bad to worse, whenever he looked
at another's property he wanted it, that was because of the piece of glass in his eye.   At last he
stole some money from a house, and was sent away
to prison and disgrace.

Now, my children, I will not stay to tell you any
more of the mischief which the evil glass did.   You
can easily understand what this parable teaches.
The devil puts bad thoughts into our minds if we
don't guard against them, and then our hearts
become hard, and cold, and selfish, and we look at
everything in a wrong way.   Sometimes Satan sends
a little bit of conceit into our heart and into our eye.
What happens then?   Why, we look at ourselves
and think how good we are, and how clever, and
how handsome.   And we look at other people, and
think what poor, common, disagreeable creatures
they are compared with us.   My children, whenever

you begin to fancy that you are better than other people, take care, examine yourselves, for there is a little bit of the Evil Spirit's glass in your heart and in your eye. Sometimes Satan sends a grain of *discontent* into your heart and eyes. Then everything looks wrong. The weather is not right, the school-lessons are too hard, the teachers are unkind, your schoolmates are disagreeable. And yet the weather, and the lessons, and the teachers, and the scholars are the same as ever. It is you who are wrong. When you are tempted to be cross, or to find fault, or to grumble, remember this parable, and ask God to give you a clean heart and a right spirit, for Jesus Christ's sake.

SERMON XV.

THE CITY OF THE GREAT KING.

PSALM XLVIII. 2.

"The City of the Great King."

A LITTLE boy once lived in a deep valley surrounded by lofty mountains. The valley lay so low that it was always covered with fog and mist, which made its roads very wet and dirty. Most of the people who lived there were quite contented with their home, and had no wish to go anywhere else, or rise above the mists and fog. It was not so with the little boy. He longed to get out of the dark, thick atmosphere, and the wet, muddy roads of the valley. He would often ask his neighbours what place there was beyond the high mountains above them. Some people said that they did not know, nor care, the valley was good enough for them. Others told him that beyond the highest mountain was the City of the Great King, which stood in perfect beauty far above the mists and darkness of the valley. Then the little boy looked longingly at the great mountains which rose up into the air, and thought to himself, "Oh! that I could climb up above the fog and darkness, and breathe the fresh mountain air, and see the City of the Great King." His neighbours only laughed at him, and told him that he was far too small and weak to climb the steep mountains, or to find his way to the beautiful city. One night the child went to sleep with his thoughts full of the City of the Great King. In his sleep he thought a bright and shining figure stood beside him, which smiled lovingly on him, and asked him what he desired most. And the wondering child answered that he wished to climb up above the mists of the valley, and see the City of the Great King. And the shining visitor again smiled lovingly upon the child, and told him that it was a good wish. But he warned him that the way was long, and steep, and difficult, and that there were many dangers in the road; but if the child would bravely climb on to the end, the stranger promised that he should enter through the gates into the city, and see the King in His beauty. Then said the angel, "The Great King knows you already, and has held you in His arms." The little boy wondered greatly how the King could know a little child like him, or when He could have held him in His arms. Then the angel told the child that when he was a little infant, he had been brought to one of the palaces of the Great King, who had received him there, and set a mark upon his forehead, and that the King knew His people wherever they were, because they bore about in their bodies His mark. All this was very wonderful to the little boy, and he longed to begin his journey, and to climb the high mountain. The angel promised to go with him, and to help him in time of need.

Well, the child went to the foot of the mountain, which rose up high into the air, and its top quite hidden from sight. At first the little boy could see no path up the mountain side; but, presently, when he went down on his knees, he was able to see the way, which was very narrow. The child had brought with him many things which he loved well, clothes, and toys, and presents from his neighbours. But he found that their weight dragged him back, and that he kept slipping from the mountain path into the misty valley. So he said, "I cannot go with these," and he cast away the weight, and began to climb once more. Then it seemed to the child that he could hear the voice of the angel at his side, although he could not see his shining form, and the voice said to him, "Go up higher, be humble, be brave, be faithful, look up, and look not back, and He shall give His angels charge concerning thee." So the child climbed on. He was often tempted to look back at the misty valley, and the houses of his neighbours, but he remembered the angel's warning —*look up, and look not back*, and lifted his eyes towards the top of the mountain above him.

There were many difficulties in the child's way, and the path was very steep and stony. At times the road was hard to find, and the child thought he had missed it altogether. Then he noticed that there were foot-prints in the way, as though some one had travelled over that same road before him. The foot-marks seemed to be those of some one who had suffered pain, for they were stained with blood. Wondering more and more, the child climbed on, and found that if he placed his feet in the marks of those other feet, the journey became easier. At length he reached a gate which stood in the path, and as the child knelt humbly before it, waiting till it should be opened to him, suddenly he saw One standing there, who looked lovingly upon him, and laid His hands upon his head, and whispered, " My strength is sufficient for thee, go up higher."

And the kneeling child saw that the Hands which were laid upon his head had wounds in them, and that His Feet were pierced, and stained with blood, then he understood whose were the foot-prints which he had followed. So the child passed through the gate, and climbed on, higher and higher. Often and often he could see the form of Him of the pierced Hands and Feet, showing him the way, and when the road was more than ever difficult, those wounded Hands were stretched out to help the child. Sometimes the child was very weary and faint, then He of the pierced Hands would come to him, and give him wonderful food, such as he had never seen in the lowly valley.

Sometimes the child would despair, thinking that he should never reach the City of the Great King. Once he found himself in a dark, thick wood, where it was very difficult to see the path. The heart of the child was very heavy, and he was half inclined to turn back. The branches of the trees caught hold of him, and held him back; long, clinging

weeds seized his legs and feet, and almost overthrew
him. Loathsome serpents crawled and hissed
about him, and tried to drive him from the path.
Still the child struggled on, higher and higher. One
day he saw some flowers and fruit, very fair to look
on, growing a little way from the path. And the
child thought—how I should like to taste that
sweet fruit, and to twist those fair flowers into gar-
lands. He forgot the angel's charge—*look up, and
turn not back*, and he turned from the path, to seek
the fruit and flowers. But when he had eaten of
the fruits, and crowned his head with blossoms, the
child felt sick and sorrowful. His eyes were dimmed,
and his brain confused, and he could not find the
path, nor see the foot-prints. He wandered about
sadly, and found that he was going *down* the mountain, instead of upwards. At last he came to a
gate, which stopped his way. Weeping bitterly,
the child knelt, bewailing his folly, while the
withered flowers fell neglected from his brow. Presently the gate was opened and the weeping child
saw that the Hand which held it was marked with
wounds, which seemed to bleed afresh. So the
child passed through the gate, and once more found
the right path. And now he looked neither to the
right hand, nor to the left, but went straight for-

ward, higher, higher still. And soon from the
mountain top there shone a bright and glorious
light, which made the child's path clear as noonday.
And the child rejoiced, for he knew that he must
be coming near to the City of the Great King.

At length he drew near to another gate, which
barred his way, and he was very weary with his
journey. So the child lay down to rest beside this
gate, and presently fell asleep. And as he slept, it
seemed to him that the angel, who had appeared
to him in the valley, once more stood beside him,
and led him tenderly through the open door.
And the child, scarce knowing whether he dreamed
or no, found himself standing in a wondrous fair
and stately city, whose light was as that of a stone
most precious. He could see gardens bright with
flowers, such as he had never seen in the misty
valley, and could hear the music of many voices,
which came to him "like the sound of a great
Amen." The streets were full of people, and there
came many children there among the rest. And
although the child had expected to feel lonely and
strange, yet the people looked upon him with
smiling faces, and there were among them some
whom he recognised as old friends. After a while,
the angel led him to One who stood waiting to

receive him, One clothed in a wondrous, shining garment, and having a crown upon His Head. The child approached timidly, not knowing what to do. And He who wore the crown, stretched forth His Hands to the child, and he saw that the Hands bore the marks of wounds. Then the child knew Him who had been his Guide, and he fell at His feet, and worshipped. And then he heard a voice speaking to him with exceeding sweetness and love, and saying to him, "Come unto Me you who labour, and are heavy laden, and I will give you rest." And there came upon the child a feeling of perfect rest and peace, the peace of God which passeth all understanding.

I think, my children, you can easily understand the meaning of this parable. The City of the Great King is Heaven, and we all have to take our journey upwards, because "here we have no continuing city, but we seek one to come." Here we are "strangers and pilgrims." We must not be content to live a selfish life, or an idle life, or a life made up of eating and drinking and playing. Such a life is all amongst the fogs and mists of the low valley. The little boy, of whom I told you, was bidden to go up higher. So are we all. We are told to "seek those things that are above, to set our affection on things in Heaven, not on things in the earth." You need not go out of the world to do this, you must live in the world, but above its sins and follies. That is what I meant by climbing the mountain, above the mists of the valley. Every one of us is going up or down, growing better or worse. If you want to see the City of the Great King, you must climb, and God will send His holy angel to help you on the journey.

The child could only find the path when he went on his knees. That teaches us that we must pray that God may show us the right road to Heaven, and that road is the *narrow way of holiness*, because "strait is the gate, and narrow is the way, which leadeth unto life." You know who trod that path before you, children ? Jesus Christ, "leaving us an example, that we should follow in His steps." The Great King first took you in His arms, and set His mark upon you, the sign of the Cross, in your Baptism. Then you will come, as the child did in the parable, to a gate, which Jesus will open for you, the gate of Holy Confirmation. You will find, too, as the child found, that you must not overload yourselves with worldly goods if you want to climb. I don't mean that you are not to have any toys, or games, or pleasures, but I *do* mean that

you must not think too much of them, you must
set God first, " Seek ye *first* the Kingdom of God
and His righteousness." Do you remember the
charge which the angel gave to the child ? " Look
up, and look *not* back." Yes, and our Saviour
gives us all the same charge, "No man having put
his hand to the plough, and looking back, is fit for
the Kingdom of God." After the child had passed
through the gate of Confirmation, He who went
before him, with pierced Hands and Feet, fed him
with wonderful food. You, my children, know
what that Food is, the Body and Blood of Jesus in
the Blessed Sacrament,whereby we are strengthened
for the journey from earth to Heaven. Once, you
remember, the child found himself in a dark wood,
where the trees and weeds clung to him. We all
have to pass such a dark place, and to meet with
things which hinder us on our journey, and these
things are the temptations of the world, the flesh,
and the devil. · Once the child strayed from the
path, and lost it, because he longed for the flowers
and fruit growing near him. My children, there
are many such flowers and fruits in the world, to
tempt you from the right path. Things which seem
very pleasant to you, but which are not *right*. Bad
company, bad talk, bad books, bad places of amuse-

ment, these will all come in your way as you grow
older; but remember if you choose them, *you lose
the path to Heaven.* Can you tell me what that
gate was through which the child passed, after he
had bitterly sorrowed for his sin? That gate was
repentance, since "if we confess our sins, He is
faithful and just to forgive us our sins, and to
cleanse us from all unrighteousness."

The last gate through which the child passed was
the gate of death, which lies before us all. God
grant, my children, that we may all so try to walk
in the right way, that when death comes, it may be
only like a sleep after a long journey, and that the
Holy Angels may bear us to the City of the Great
King, and to the presence of that dear Saviour who
was wounded for our transgressions, who rose again
for our justification, and who has gone up on high
to prepare a place for us.

SERMON XVI.

THE LIVING BOOK.

----

1 SAMUEL III. 9.

"Speak, Lord, for Thy servant heareth."

THERE is an old fairy story, which some of you, my
children, may remember. It tells us of one who
possessed a magic ring, which enabled him to understand the language of birds and beasts. Now I
have often wished for such a ring. I should dearly
like to understand what the birds in the hedges are
saying to one another. I am quite sure that birds
do talk to each other, and that dogs, and cows, and
horses, and all animals, have their secrets, which
they whisper into each other's ears.

Well, I am going to tell you about a child who
fancied he could understand the language of the birds
and beasts about him.   He was not strong and
healthy enough to play with other children, so he was
much alone, and that made him very thoughtful. He
was never tired of studying nature, and learning about
flowers, and trees, and animals ; and from being so
much with them, and so seldom with any other company, the child learned to find " Tongues in trees,
books in the running brooks, sermons in stones, and
good in everything." The child had read how the good
Saint Francis used to call the birds and beasts his
brethren, how he called the lark his sister ; and how,
when he was dying, the Saint whispered—" Welcome, sister death." The child thought all this very
beautiful, as indeed it is ; and he loved to find his
brethren and playmates in God's world of nature.
The child would think to himself—"I am too weakly
to play and run with other children, and they do
not care for my talk.   But the skylark can tell me
what the world looks like from the blue sky, and the
bees, as they go humming by, bring me sweet messages from the woods and meadows.   I soon grow
tired of hearing people talk, it makes my head ache.
But I am never weary of the river, that tells me
such wonderful stories !"   Now, most people only

heard the stream murmuring among the reeds, or
rushing over the stones; but to the child the river
spoke a language which he could understand. It
told him how it was born in a little spring, far away
among the hills, and how at first it was only a baby
of a stream, and how it grew bigger and stronger,
and carried ships and men far out to the wide sea.
Sometimes the child was taken to the sea-side, and
there indeed he had friends to talk with. The
winds and the waves brought all kinds of messages.
Sometimes the wind seemed to tell him that it had
come from Africa, and had been blowing over wide
deserts of yellow sand, and dark, hot jungle. Sometimes a fresh, cool wind would come blowing across
the sea, which seemed to bring the child a message
from the North, and he could see in fancy, snow-
crowned mountains, and dark pine-woods, and lakes
of glittering ice. If he put a sea-shell to his ear, the
child would say that the shell was telling the secrets
of the sea, and reminding him of Columbus, and
Drake, and Raleigh, and many another good sea-
king of olden time. And the child would often say
that God had been talking to him. And when his
friends asked him how this was possible, the child
would answer that God spoke to him by His Works.
The wind roaring in the Autumn made the child

remember "how God doth send forth His voice, yea, and that a mighty voice ; the voice of the Lord shaketh the wilderness of Cades."   When the Autumn leaves fell thick around him, the child seemed to hear the voice of God whispering—" We all do fade as a leaf. We fade away suddenly like the grass : in the morning it is green, and groweth up, but in the evening it is cut down, dried up, and withered." When the buds peeped out in valley and hedgerow in the spring time, the child seemed to hear God's voice on every side, saying, "I am the Resurrection and the Life ; He that sitteth upon the throne maketh all things new."   So it seemed that God spoke to the little boy.   In the child's home there was a great library of books, and when he could not go out, he spent his time in reading. It seemed to him that the people in his favourite books were all living, and that they spoke to him. All the characters in the dear old fairy tales, and children's stories, were real living companions to the. lonely child.   They could take him away from the room where he sat, and make him forget his weak health, and his solitary life.   One day, he was away in a lonely, tropical island, with Robinson Crusoe, or Sindbad the Sailor, amongst brilliant birds, and glorious fruits and flowers.   He could fly away in a minute to China, and see Aladdin's palace, and the wonderful lamp. So, too, all the persons in history seemed alive to the child, and appeared to walk out of the pages of the book, as it were. When he read of the Norman Conquest, he did not think of it as having happened eight hundred years ago, but only yesterday. The child fancied he could hear the tramp of feet as the Normans rushed up the hill at Hastings, and the whistling of the arrows, and and the clash of the battle-axes round King Harold, and the standard.

But there was one book which the child loved best, and which he always called his *living Book*. That book was the Bible, and he was never tired of reading it. " They are all alive to me," he would say of the Scripture characters. " I can see them, and hear them talk, and then God speaks to me as He did to the child Samuel, and I answer, " Speak, Lord, for Thy servant heareth." It seemed to the child as if he knew Samuel as a boy of his own age, and as though they walked together in the house of the Lord as friends. He had cried over the death of the Shunammite's son, and rejoiced at his return to life, just as if these two children had known each other, and played together in the corn fields. But there was One Child whom the little boy loved to think of, and to look at oftener than any other. When he read of Him, there seemed to rise before him a little town among the hills; a fair place, where the red cactus and many another flower grew wild. Among the children in the bright Easter dresses, who played among the hills, or rested by the fountains, there was One whose face seemed more beautiful than the others, who, though He played with the children, was often grave and thoughtful. The little boy loved to follow every step of that Holy Child, through all the wondrous, beautiful story. He would picture the gentle, patient, loving life of the Child Jesus, and then pray that he might be gentle, and patient, and loving too. He tried to do as a famous Saint advises us, " to be little with the Ltttle One, that we may increase in stature with Him," by setting before him the example of that Perfect Child who "increased in stature, and in favour with God and man ;" as pure and stainless " as the flower of roses in the spring of the year, and as lilies by the waters."

So it was that the Bible was to the child a living book. He could see the workshop at Nazareth, and the Boy Jesus helping Joseph at his bench. He could see the gentle mother watching her Son with thought-ful eyes, and wondering how the words of the prophets should be fulfilled. He could see the Holy Child going for the first time to Jerusalem, along the road edged by fields of dazzling green, and spangled with a thousand flowers. He could see the spacious halls of the Temple, and watch the Child Jesus standing among the doctors.

As each holy season of the Church's year came round, it seemed to the little boy that what had happened so long ago was actually taking place. When he went to Church on Christmas Day, he fancied himself in the rocky stable among the Bethlehem hills. When the bells pealed out in the quiet winter air, the child could hear the angels' song, "Peace on earth, good will towards men." At Epiphany, the little boy would look up at the sky, and among the stars he would find one which appeared to him the very same which had guided the wise men with their gifts. Lent would carry the child's thoughts into the wilderness, and he actually seemed to look on the Lord kneeling in that lonely place, faint with long fasting, and bowed with many sorrows. Day by day in Holy Week the child would follow Jesus, step by step. He could see the dark olive trees shading the sad Garden of Gethsemane. He could look on the disciples sleeping, whilst the Lord knelt in agony. He could hear

the voices of the crowd of armed men, as they broke
into the garden, and see the glare of the torches,
and the flashing sword of S. Peter.   It appeared
to the child that when Jesus was led away, he followed, and shrank back from the pale, trembling
traitor, Judas.   The angry voices in Pilate's hall
sounded distinctly in his ears, and that savage cry
" Crucify Him, crucify Him."   On Good Friday,
the child fancied himself at Calvary.   He would
shudder at the brutal talk of the soldiers, as they
gambled for the seamless robe beneath the Cross.
The crowds of strangers thronging Jerusalem, the
awful darkness and stillness at Calvary, the bitter
cry of Jesus from the Cross, all these things were to
the child quite real and present.   Then the sweet
Eastertide would come, and the child would think—
I must go to the Garden, and look at the Sepulchre.
And he would fancy, as he knelt among the flowers
in Church, that he was really among the lilies in
Joseph's garden, and that Jesus was standing by the
empty tomb, speaking to Mary Magdalene.   Ascen-
sion day showed the child the same Jesus, going up
to His Heavenly Home, and stretching out His
Hands to bless, and on Whit-Sunday he could hear
the sound of the mighty rushing wind, as the Holy
Spirit came down upon the place.

So the child lived with the people of whom he read. If he felt weary, he could go to Bethany, and rest with Martha and Mary, and see Jesus there. If he were weak and ailing, and laid upon his bed, Jesus seemed to stand by his side, as He stood by the side of Jairus' little daughter. If he were sad and unhappy, he could go to Gethsemane, and weep with Jesus. So it was that the child found comfort in his Bible, he could say—it is a living Book, Jesus is alive to me !

SERMON XVII.

EYES AND NO EYES.

PSALM CXXXV. 16.

" Eyes have they, but they see not."

THAT is very true of a great many people. "They
have eyes, but they see not." David was thinking
of the idols of the heathen when he wrote the text.
He says the idols have eyes, and ears, and noses,
but cannot use them, and that they who make them
and worship them are in the same condition. Now
I am not going to talk about the heathen, or their
idols, but about Christian children. We have all
got eyes, but we do not all know how to use them.
Some of us are like those of whom our Lord said,
" O blind, and slow of heart."

The Greeks have an old fable about Argus, who had one hundred eyes. I suppose they meant that he was very watchful. We have only two eyes, but they are quite sufficient if we use them properly. I dare say, children, you have heard this advice given to a young man beginning life in the world, "keep your eyes open, and you will succeed." It is very good advice. If you want to get on in life you must keep your eyes open, you must look about you, you must be ready, when you see your chance, to take it. But I want you to use your eyes for a better purpose than this. Do you know there is a certain water-beetle which has two sets of eyes; with one pair it looks down into the water, with the other pair it looks upward? Now whilst I want you to use your eyes for your advantage, that you may see your way to success, I want you to use them in a far higher and better way, in looking for God. If you ask me *where* you are to look for God, I answer, everywhere. Look for God in this beautiful world. I heard of a little girl once, who said, "I wish I had grandfather's eyes." When she was asked why she wished for the eyes of an old man, who was obliged to wear spectacles, she answered, "that if she saw with her grandfather's eyes, whenever she walked in the fields and lanes she would

see God's goodness in everything." There are some
people who walk about in the country, and never
see anything of God. They look at the flowers,
and only think of them as the savage did, as being
" weeds which smell." They hear the birds singing, and their only idea is to throw a stone at the
bird, or to rob its nest. It is the old story of *Eyes
and No Eyes* over again. If we use our sight properly, we shall see the wisdom, and power, and love
of God in every blade of grass, in every yellow
cornfield, in every laden orchard, in the spring
flower and the autumn wood, we shall see that God
has "made everything beautiful in his time." I
suppose all of you children have noticed a pretty
little blue flower which grows all over our banks
and hedges. It is called *Veronica*, and there is a
beautiful legend about a saint of that name. When
the Lord Jesus was on His sad way to Crucifixion,
He fainted under the weight of His Cross. Among
all the crowd of people who watched Him, none
offered to help the suffering Saviour except one
maiden. She went forward, and wiped the Lord's
face with a napkin, and then she found that the
image, or picture, of Christ's features was printed
on the cloth. Now if we use our eyes in the right
way, when we look at the blue Veronica, or any

other flower, we shall see a picture of the dear
Lord who made all things bright and beautiful.
There is another flower which some of you have
seen, called the Passion Flower. It gets its name
from our Lord's sufferings, because people fancy
they see in it the marks of Christ's wounds. Now
every flower can show you something, or tell you
something, about Jesus and the love of God. Suppose you are sitting before a bright fire in the
winter time. You see how red the coals are, and
feel the pleasant heat which they send out. Well,
if you use your eyes rightly, you will see God's
wonderful hand there. How do you suppose that
heat got into the hard black coal? It is God's sunshine coming out. Thousands of years ago, where
the coal pits are now, there were great forest trees
growing. The sunshine flashed warm and golden
on those trees year after year, and the trees
breathed it in day after day. Then the great trees
were buried for ages, and became coal, and the
sunshine and heat of thousands of years ago is
coming out of the coal now to warm you. See how
God takes care of us all.

Some of you children have a little baby brother
or sister. You know that at first the baby never
seems to look at anything, it merely eats and sleeps.

I

But after a time the baby begins to look round, and to hold out its hands to the light, and to laugh when you play with it.   Then people say the baby begins to *take notice*.   Now I want all of you children to use your eyes, and to *take notice*.   When you read your Bible, *take notice*.   I have seen people go to one of our great museums and picture galleries, and they walked through room after room, and passed by picture after picture, and yet showed no interest.   They were not blind people, they had eyes, but they saw not, they did not take notice. Many people read the Bible in the same way.

The Bible is full of pictures, but some of you never find them out.   The Bible is full of beauty, yet some of you have only found it dry, dull reading.   When you next open your Bible, use your eyes, take notice.   Look for the pictures of Jesus everywhere.   When you read of Abel, killed beside his sacrifice by his brother Cain, look for the likeness of Jesus, who was killed by His brethren, and offered as a sacrifice for the sins of the whole world. When you read of Joshua sent to lead the children of Israel into the promised land, look for the picture of Jesus, whose name, like Joshua, means a Saviour, and who came to lead us into the good Land of Heaven.   When you hear of Noah and his family saved from perishing in the ark by water, think how Jesus saves us. Our ark is the Church, and the water of baptism is the means of our salvation.

I wonder what sort of eyes we must have to see God in His works, and in His Bible. They need not be young, bright, eyes like yours. There are many dim, old, eyes, nearly blind, which can see more than those of the young. We must have *believing* eyes, eyes of *faith*, then we shall see God.

I have read a very beautiful story of a poor little girl who was leaning one cold winter night against the wall of a house. She was quite alone in the snowy street, it was Christmas time, and most people were gathered at the cheerful fireside. The child was quite friendless, and without a home, and she held a box of matches in her poor cold hands. She had tried to sell them, but no one would buy.

Shivering in the wintry wind, she struck a match against the wall of the house, hoping to warm herself. Then a very wonderful thing happened. The match burned bright and strong as a candle, and gave out a pleasant warmth, so that the child fancied she was sitting before a real fire burning in a polished stove. She stretched her bare cold feet to warm them too, when the match went out, and the bright fire vanished, and there was only the cold stone wall before her.

Well, the little girl rubbed another match on the wall, and immediately the wall became transparent, like glass, and she could see into the room. There was a party of happy children gathered round their parents, and the dark green holly was shining with red berries, and there were sounds of music and merry laughter. Then the match went out, and all was darkness.

Again she rubbed a match upon the wall, and the child saw a splendid Christmas tree, hundreds of lights burned upon it, and pretty presents hung from the branches. Just as the little girl stretched out her hand towards the tree, the match went out, and all was hidden.

Once more she rubbed a match upon the wall, and now she seemed to be looking into a Church lighted up for service. She saw the Altar with its white hangings and fair flowers. She saw a text stretching across the wall—"Unto us a Child is born"—she seemed to hear the sound of many voices chanting

> " Hark ! the herald angels sing,
>   Glory to the new-born King."

Then she fancied that one of these Angels was coming towards her, dressed in glittering white. The little girl cried to the angel to take her, and hold her fast, for she knew that the bright picture would vanish away like the room, and the Christmas tree ; and she made haste to strike all the bundle of matches. Then the light grew very brilliant, and it seemed as though the angel took the child in his arms, and carried her away from the dreary, dark street, never to know cold or hunger again. In the morning people found the little girl lying against the wall with a smile on her face, frozen to death. She was still holding the bundle of burnt matches, and the people said she had tried to warm herself. But no one dreamed of the wonderful things she had seen, and how the Angel had carried her to keep Christmas with Jesus. My children, I think you would all like to have those wonderful matches.

Well, if you have the eye of faith you can see Heaven opened, and the holy Angels watching about your path and about your bed, and waiting to carry you one day from the Church on earth to the Church in Paradise.

Well, I have told you that if you want to see God's Hand in Nature, and the Bible, you must look with the eye of faith. Next, I want you to look at things and people with the eye of *love*. Things

appear so different when looked at in different lights.
To a person who is suffering from liver complaint .
everything looks yellow.   To a person looking out
of a dirty window everything looks black and ugly.
I want you to use your eyes in looking out for the
good in people.   If you take your watch to a watch-
maker and tell him that it won't go, he opens the
works of the watch, and puts a strong magnifying
glass in his eye, and looks about till he finds what
is wrong.   A little speck of dust has got under one
wheel, or a little pin has come loose, and the watch
won't go.   My children, some people are always
putting a magnifying glass into their eye, and looking into their neighbour's works to find out something wrong.   Children do it, men and women do it.
You remember how our Lord Jesus Christ reproved
people for doing this.   He says we must first cast
the beam out of our own eye before we can see
clearly to cast the mote out of our brother's eye.
Children, look out for your own faults, that will give
you quite enough to do.

A wise man of old says that everyone carries two
bags with him, one hanging before him, another
behind him.   Into the bag in front he puts the faults
of others, into that behind he puts his own.   By
that means he always sees his neighbour's failings,

and never sees his own. If you want to be happy, my children, look out for the good in others. The fault-finder, the mischief-maker, are never happy, and no one loves them. Remember there are two ways of looking at things.

I dare say you have heard the story of the two knights and the shield? Two knights in armour were riding along a road from opposite directions, when they suddenly saw a shield hanging up by the road side. One of the knights exclaimed, " what a splendid golden shield ! " The other answered him, " you must be blind, the shield is of silver." The first knight insisted that the shield was made of gold, and at last they quarrelled over the matter, and began to fight. Presently a stranger came up, and asked what they were fighting about. " This man," said the first knight, " declares that this shield is made of silver, whilst I can see that it is gold." " Foolish men," answered the stranger, " you are both right, and both wrong : look on both sides of the shield." Then the knights saw that one side of the shield was of gold, the other of silver.

Children, always look on *both sides*, and never be hasty to judge another.

THE END.

Lightning Source UK Ltd.
Milton Keynes UK
UKHW022225160519
342828UK00007B/212/P